MANGA

HUNTER × HUNTER

ハンター × ハンター

Story & Art by

Yoshihiro Togashi

Volume 17

CHARACTERS

Gon

OUR EAGER HERO. NOW A HUNTER, HE'S ON A SEARCH TO REUNITE WITH HIS FATHER!

The Story Thus Far

GON DREAMS OF BEING A HUNTER LIKE THE FATHER HE HARDLY REMEMBERS, THE GREAT GING FREECSS. HE PASSES THE HIGHLY SELECTIVE LICENSING EXAM, BUT FINDING GING WILL BE EVEN HARDER.

ONE OF THE CLUES GING LEFT BEHIND IS A MEMORY CARD FOR THE HUNTER-ONLY GAME, "GREED ISLAND." GON AND KILLUA START PLAYING, BUT THERE'S NOTHING EASY IN THIS GAME GING MADE WITH HIS FRIENDS. THEY STUDY THE FINER POINTS OF NEN UNDER BISCUIT'S TUTELAGE.

MEANWHILE, THE BOMBERS RESORT TO VIOLENT MEANS AS THEY APPROACH COMPLETION OF THE GAME. GON AND HIS FRIENDS ASSEMBLE A TEAM TO ACQUIRE A CARD NOBODY ELSE HAS, THE "PLOT OF BEACH," AND CHALLENGE RAZOR, ONE OF THE GAME MASTERS. HOW WILL THEY FARE...?!

Killua
GON'S FRIEND. ON A JOURNEY WITH GON TO FIND WHAT HE WANTS TO DO WITH HIS LIFE.
Tsezguerra
A SINGLE-STAR PRO HUNTER, HE TEAMS UP WITH GON TO THWART THE BOMBER.
Biscuit
A 57-YEAR-OLD PRO HUNTER, SHE SEES POTENTIAL IN GON AND KILLUA.
Hisoka
A CREEPY MAGICIAN WHO THINKS OF GON AS PREY. HE CAME TO GREED ISLAND LOOKING FOR AN EXORCIST.
Genthru
A.K.A. "THE BOMBER." HIS ABILITIES ARE COUNTDOWN AND LITTLE FLOWER.

HUNTER×HUNTER

Volume 17

CONTENTS

KAWHAM
BOOYAH!! SEE HOW YOU LIKE IT BEING OUT!!
GSH ?!
PLUS, IT'LL BE OUR BALL...
RAZOR WILL USE "BACK" TO COME BACK IN PLAY ANYWAY... AT LEAST WE MADE HIM USE IT UP EARLY.

Chapter 164 Face-Off: Part 7

SHF
TMP
ZOOM
WHA-?
WHAP!!

WSH
WHAP!
TMP
UH...
...
BAM

WHAP!!
DOOMM
GO-
GOREINU!!
NICE ABILITY.
NURTURE IT WELL.
TWIK
HEY, YOU! THAT WAS UNCALLED FOR!!
HM?
THERE'S NO RULE AGAINST PASSING TO THE OPPOSING TEAM.
HEAD SHOTS ARE LEGAL, TOO.
IF THAT BALL HAD HIT THE FLOOR, I WOULD'VE BEEN OUT.
FSSSH

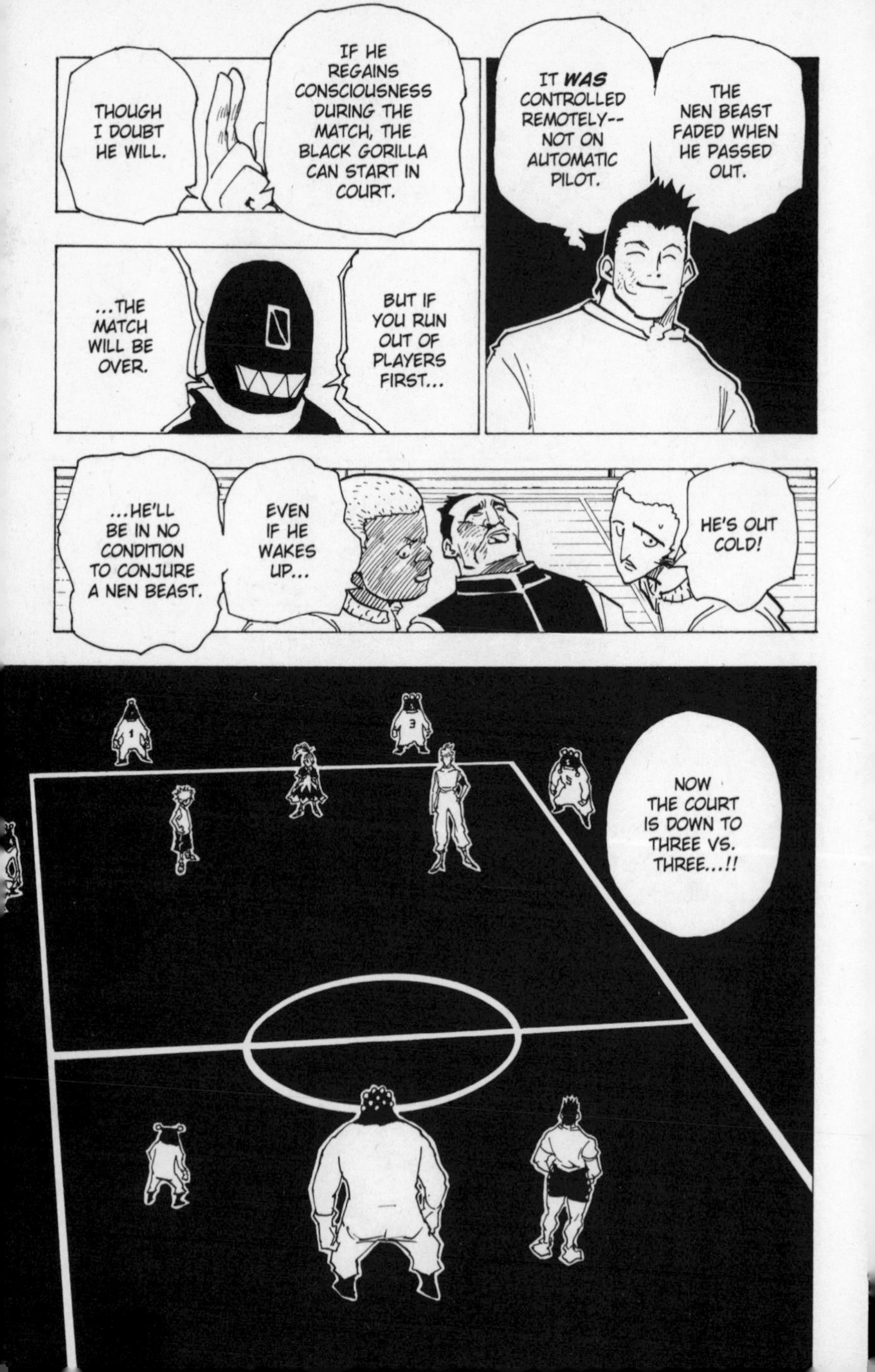
THE NEN BEAST FADED WHEN HE PASSED OUT.
IT **WAS** CONTROLLED REMOTELY-- NOT ON AUTOMATIC PILOT.
IF HE REGAINS CONSCIOUSNESS DURING THE MATCH, THE BLACK GORILLA CAN START IN COURT.
THOUGH I DOUBT HE WILL.
BUT IF YOU RUN OUT OF PLAYERS FIRST...
...THE MATCH WILL BE OVER.
HE'S OUT COLD!
EVEN IF HE WAKES UP...
...HE'LL BE IN NO CONDITION TO CONJURE A NEN BEAST.
NOW THE COURT IS DOWN TO THREE VS. THREE...!!

HALF OF US ARE NOW SITTING OUT, WITH ONE INJURED KID AS THE RETRIEVER.
BUT THE PRESSURE'S MORE ON US.
THE ENEMY'S MANY RETRIEVERS CAN ATTACK FROM ANYWHERE.
GSH...
RAZOR IS STILL IN COURT, HIS FREE OUT UNUSED.
WE'RE AT A SERIOUS DISADVANTAGE!!
AND THEY HAVE CONTROL OF THE BALL...!!
NOW THEN...
SH
HS
SHF
WHO...
FSH
...WILL GO NEXT?!

DOOOOM
IT'S COMING TO *ME!!* NOW WHAT?!
I CAN'T CATCH THIS!!
SHF
I HAVE TO DODGE...
SHOOOM
!!

IT CURVED?!!
A SHOOT BALL?!

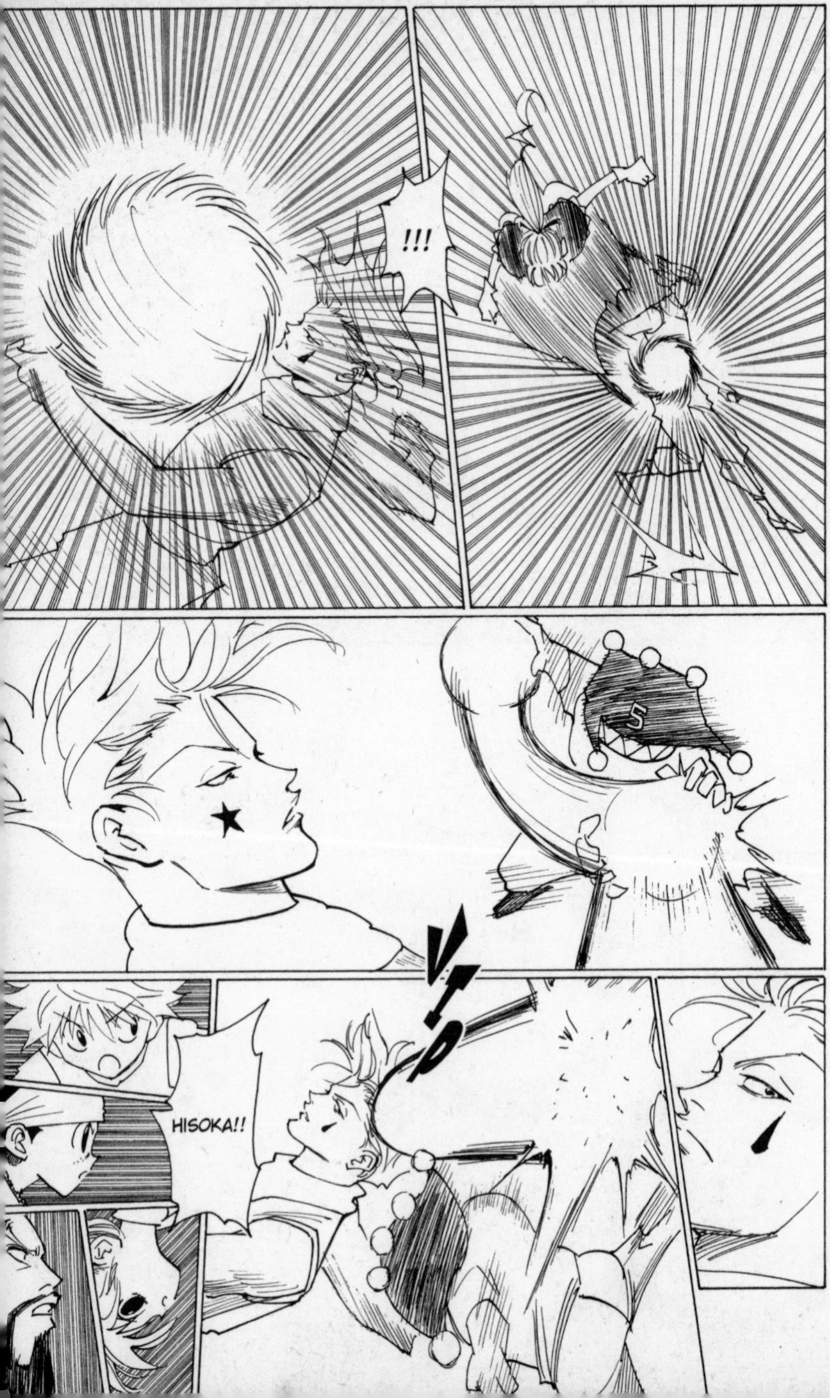
!!!
VIP
HISOKA!!

BUNGEE GUM!!
SPLAT!!
SHKKK!!
RAZOR MADE IT SEEM LIKE IT WAS COMING FOR ME...
VMM...
...WHEN HIS REAL GOAL WAS NAILING BISCUIT AND HISOKA AT ONCE...!!

BUT I COULD'VE JUST AS EASILY DUCKED TO THE LEFT...!!
THEN I WOULDN'T HAVE BEEN ABLE TO ESCAPE...!!
GRR
BISCUIT IS OUT!!
STEP OUT OF THE COURT!!
WHAT?!
WHY?!
CLOTHING COUNTS...
IS THAT HOW IT IS?
DRAT.
AND I THOUGHT SHE WAS SAFE...
ONLY TWO LEFT! YOU CAN'T LET THEM GET CONTROL OF THE BALL!!
BACK!!

SHF
GON DECLARES, "BACK"!!
HE MOVES BACK ON THE COURT!!
CAN THAT KID REALLY HANDLE IT?
HE'S NOT JUST ANY KID.
HE'S THE ONLY ONE WHO WENT HEAD TO HEAD AGAINST RAZOR'S BALL.

ARE YOU O.K.?
YEAH.
DON'T OVERDO IT, YOU HEAR?
YEAH.
...
WHAT'S 1+1?
YEAH.
GO ON, BEAT HIM IF IT KILLS YOU!!
HOPELESS.
I WILL!!
YOU OKAY?
I'M FINE!
I FOUND OUT ONE THING. ♣
THE BALL IS LESS DESTRUCTIVE ONCE IT PASSES THROUGH A RETRIEVER. ♦
I ONLY BROKE TWO FINGERS, WITHOUT KO. ♥
SO WE WON'T GET HURT AS LONG AS WE DODGE RAZOR'S THROWS.
RIGHT. ♦
KRAK
POP
THAT WON'T BE A TRUE VICTORY!

WHAT?
A WIN IS A WIN! WE GOTTA BE ABLE TO WIN AT ALL BEFORE YOU CAN GET PICKY!
CALM DOWN!
DOESN'T IT MAKE YOU FEEL ANGRY?
SAY WHAT?!
IF YOU HAD DODGED TO THE LEFT, YOU WOULD'VE BEEN DEAD.
!
RIGHT?
I'M REALLY BOILING INSIDE.
KRAK
A CHEAP WIN WON'T BE GOOD ENOUGH!
I HAVE TO CRUSH HIM COMPLETELY!!"

YOU GOT AN IDEA?
YUP.
I'LL SHOW YOU.
KILLUA.
STAND THERE.
BEND YOUR KNEES AND HOLD THE BALL.
HUH? OKAY.
!
OF COURSE!
GMP
SHOW ME...
ROCK!!

28: CAPRICIOUS REMOTE (B - 27)	A REMOTE CONTROL TO MANIPULATE TEN EMOTIONS SOMEONE FEELS TOWARD SOMEONE ELSE, ON AN INTENSITY SCALE OF 1-10. (YOU CANNOT CONTROL HOW PEOPLE FEEL TOWARD YOU.)
29: PRE-ORDER VOUCHERS (A - 10)	WRITE THE NAME OF ANY COMMERCIALLY AVAILABLE PRODUCT ON A VOUCHER AND YOU'LL BE GUARANTEED TO GET IT REGARDLESS OF ITS SCARCITY (YOU STILL HAVE TO PAY). A BOOK OF 1000.
30: FAVOR CUSHION (B - 21)	SEAT SOMEONE ON THIS CUSHION AND HE WILL DO ONE THING FOR YOU, SO LONG AS IT IS WITHIN HIS CAPABILITIES.
31: DOUBLE POSTCARD TO THE DEAD (S - 13)	ADDRESS AND MAIL THIS RETURN POSTAGE-PAID POSTCARD TO A DECEASED PERSON, AND YOU WILL GET A REPLY THE NEXT DAY. A BOOK OF 1000.
32: PARROT CANDY (B - 30)	SUCKING ON THIS CANDY ENABLES YOU TO PRODUCE ANY VOICE. THE EFFECT LASTS UNTIL YOU NEXT INGEST SOMETHING. A SET OF 10 PACKS, 50 CANDIES PER PACK.
33: HORMONE COOKIES (S - 13)	AFTER EATING THIS COOKIE, YOUR SEX WILL TEMPORARILY CHANGE FOR 24 HOURS. A SET OF 10 BOXES, 20 COOKIES PER BOX.
34: UNIVERSAL SURVEY (B - 30)	WRITE VARIOUS QUESTIONS PERTAINING TO YOURSELF AND GIVE IT TO SOMEONE, AND HE WILL ANSWER ALL QUESTIONS HONESTLY. REUSABLE.
35: CHAMELEON CAT (S - 8)	AN ENDANGERED SPECIES. ONCE TAMED, IT CAN TRANSFORM INTO ANY ANIMAL. HOWEVER, ITS MASS REMAINS CONSTANT, SO IT WILL BE A TINY ELEPHANT OR A LARGE HAMSTER, FOR EXAMPLE.
36: RECYCLING ROOM (S - 10)	PUT SOMETHING BROKEN IN THIS ROOM AND IT WILL BE REPAIRED AS GOOD AS NEW 24 HOURS LATER. THE DOOR MUST NOT BE OPENED UNTIL TIME IS UP.

Chapter 165
Face-Off: Part 8

ROCK!!!

BA

2
13
13

SLAM
HM!
GSH.
NO. 13 IS OUT!!
CATCHING THE BALL WHILE THE BODY IS TOUCHING OUTSIDE THE COURT IS NOT LEGAL!! GON'S TEAM HAS POSSESSION!!
OH, WOW!!!
WOOT!
HE BLEW AWAY THE BIGGEST GUY!!!

ARGH!!
THAT WASN'T GOOD ENOUGH!!
...
HE'S STILL NOT SATISFIED.
HA HA.
HE'S GOTTA HAVE SOME CRAZY STANDARDS.
THAT WON'T BE ENOUGH TO KNOCK OUT RAZOR...!!
I NEED MORE POWER...!!
!
THROB
OKAY, ANOTHER GO!!
LET'S TAKE RAZOR DOWN!
!
OKAY!

TO KNOCK OUT RAZOR...
I NEED A LOT MORE POWER!!!
VM
REN!!
M
MM

SO MUCH AURA...!!
...
YOU PICKED THE WRONG SPORT.
HE CAN TAKE ALL THE TIME HE WANTS TO BUILD UP.
YOU SHOULD GET OUT OF THE WAY.
YOU KIDDING?
TAKE THE BUILT-UP AURA AND...
SHOW ME...
FOCUS INTO MY FIST!!
ROCK!

EAT THIS, RAZOR!!
JAN!!
KEN!!!
ROCK !!!!

WHAM
PERFECT!!
HE CAN'T CATCH IT!!
SKM
!!

TUCK
A BUMP?!
HE JERKED HIS WHOLE BODY BACK...
...AND KILLED THE BALL'S MOMENTUM!!

HIS TIMING HAD TO BE PERFECT!! AND HE DEFLECTED THE FORCE SO SMOOTHLY...!!
THIS MAN IS SERIOUSLY GOOD...!!
BRR
BRR
AWESOME!
IT'S NOT ALL DODGING AND CATCHING.
NOT THAT THIS IS HELPFUL.
SHK
GON'S BALL WAS JUST AS POWERFUL AS RAZOR'S...!
BUT IT DIDN'T EVEN REACH THE CEILING...
THAT BUMP CANCELED OUT ITS MOMENTUM COMPLETELY.

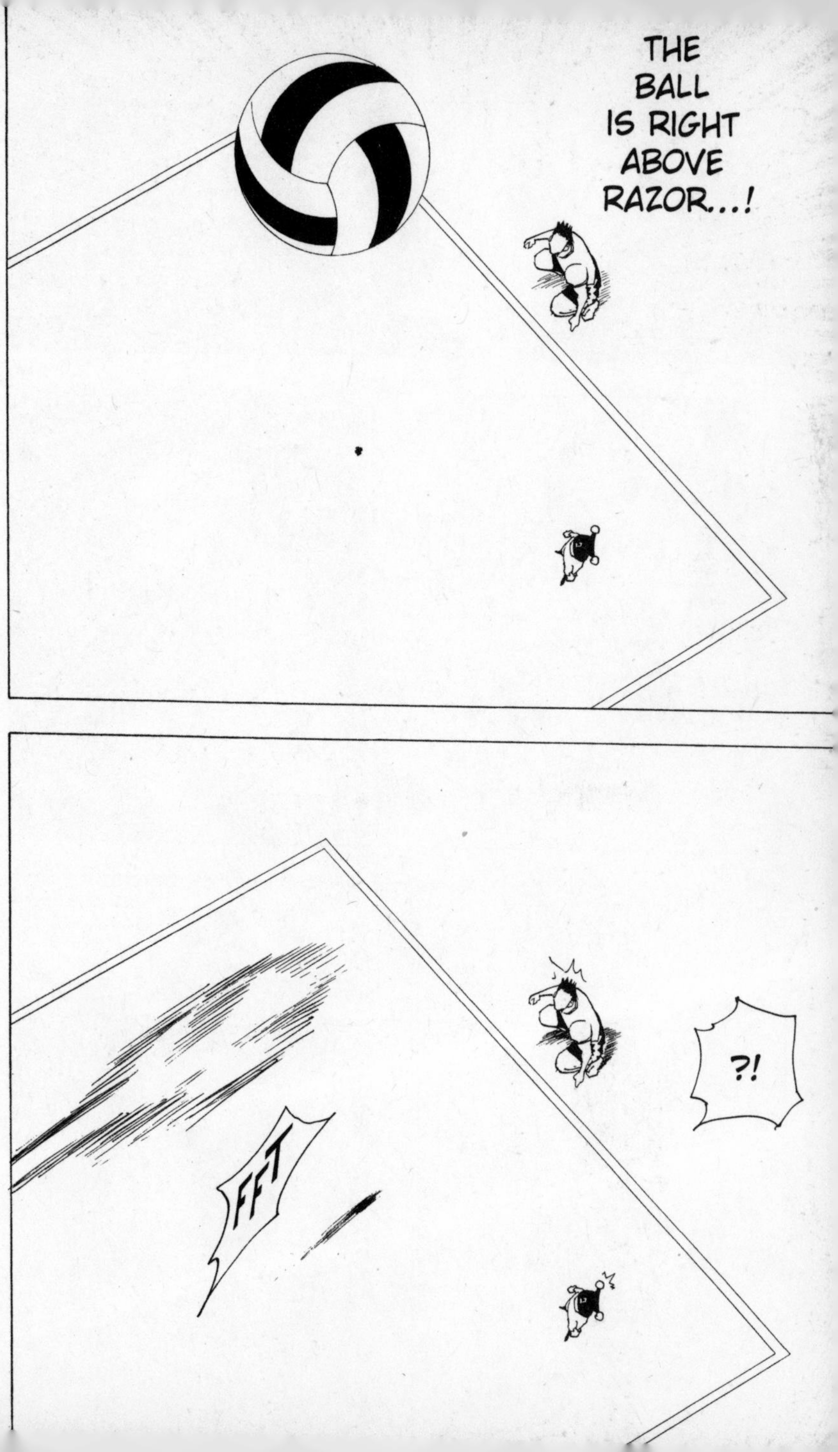
THE BALL IS RIGHT ABOVE RAZOR...!
?!
FFT

TA-DA
"ELASTIC LOVE": BUNGEE GUM!!!
TSK TSK. ♥
GOTTA HOLD ON TO THE BALL, YOU KNOW?
THE CUSHION RULE APPLIES!! RAZOR IS OUT!!
BACK...!!

37: FLEDGLING ATHLETE (B - 30)	WARM THIS MAGIC EGG IN YOUR HAND FOR THREE HOURS A DAY FOR ONE TO TEN YEARS, AND YOU WILL BECOME A TOP ATHLETE WHEN IT HATCHES. THE STRONGER YOUR DESIRE DURING INCUBATION, THE SOONER IT WILL HATCH.
38: FLEDGLING ARTIST (B - 30)	DITTO ("TOP ARTIST")
39: FLEDGLING POLITICIAN (B - 30)	DITTO ("TOP POLITICIAN")
40: FLEDGLING MUSICIAN (B - 30)	DITTO ("TOP MUSICIAN")
41: FLEDGLING PILOT (B - 30)	DITTO ("TOP PILOT")
42: FLEDGLING NOVELIST (B - 30)	DITTO ("TOP NOVELIST")
43: FLEDGLING GAMBLER (B - 30)	DITTO ("TOP GAMBLER")
44: FLEDGLING ACTOR (B - 30)	DITTO ("TOP ACTOR")
45: FLEDGLING CEO (B - 30)	DITTO ("TOP CEO")

Chapter 166
Face-Off: Part 9
SHK
RAZOR USES THE "BACK" OPTION!!
HE REMAINS ON THE COURT!!
BOTH TEAMS USED UP THE FREEBIE, AND IT'S THREE TO TWO!!
NOW THE TABLES HAVE TURNED!!
HAVE THEY?
?!
WE'RE THE ONES IN BAD SHAPE...
HISOKA PROBABLY CAN'T THROW ANYMORE.
I BET HE CAN'T EVEN *CATCH* WITH HIS RIGHT HAND.
GON USED UP ALL THAT AURA IN THE ATTACK.
HE SHOULD BE CLOSE TO EXHAUSTION...

I DOUBT HE WOULD BE ABLE TO REPRODUCE...
...THE SAME KIND OF SHOT.
SO...
KILLUA'S THE ONLY ONE WHO'S ALL RIGHT...?!
QUITE THE OPPOSITE.
HUH?!
OF THE THREE, KILLUA...
...IS THE ONE MOST GRAVELY INJURED!!
?!
WHAT DO YOU MEAN?!

READ THIS WAY

PHEW
HOW'RE YOU DOING, GON?
STILL OKAY.
BUT I THINK THE NEXT WILL BE THE LAST...
AND I'LL USE ALL I'VE GOT!!
YUP.
MAKE IT GOOD!!
ONLY ONE MORE... I'LL MANAGE!
I CAN STILL HOLD IT...!!
KILLUA ISN'T PROTECTING HIS HANDS WITH NEN WHEN GON STRIKES THE BALL.
AT ALL.
?!
BUT... IT'S LIKE A *CANNON!*
YES.
HIS BARE HANDS ARE BASICALLY ACTING AS THE BARREL FOR A CANNONBALL.

IF HE PROTECTED HIS HANDS WITH A WALL OF AURA...
...IT WOULD PREVENT THE ENERGY OF GON'S PUNCH FROM TRANSFERRING TO THE BALL.
TO MINIMIZE INTERFERENCE...
...HE'S LEAVING HIS HANDS UNPROTECTED...!
BOTH OF KILLUA'S HANDS SHOULD BE INJURED...
...MUCH WORSE THAN HISOKA'S RIGHT HAND.
I'M SUCH AN IDIOT...
WHY AM I NOT UP THERE WITH THEM...?!
I HAVE THE SKILLS KILLUA DOESN'T YET HAVE...!!
I COULD SWIFTLY SWITCH MY AURA TO MY HANDS THE INSTANT THE BALL IS FIRED...!!
WAIT A MINUTE...!!

HISOKA.
PASS ME THE BALL.
WHAP
I'M NOT THAT GOOD...
SHF
...AT THROWING...
BUT!
WHIP!!
GSH!
POW
YES!
ONLY ONE LEFT...

RAZOR!!!
M
RMM
TIME!
I HAVE A QUESTION.
CAN SOMEONE INSIDE THE COURT STEP OUTSIDE OF HIS OWN WILL?
THAT'S NO PROBLEM, BUT...
HE'LL STAY OUT.
GOOD...
COME WITH ME.

GON, IF YOU STEP OUTSIDE THE COURT...
I CAN HOLD THE BALL FOR YOU!!
KILLUA'S HANDS ARE SURELY MANGLED BY NOW.
HE WON'T BE ABLE TO SECURE THE BALL PROPERLY.
I'D BE ABLE TO TRANSFER MY AURA FAST ENOUGH!
I'LL HOLD THE BALL, SO GET RAZOR FROM OUTSIDE.
THAT'S THE ONLY WAY TO WIN...!
THAT'S NOT GOOD ENOUGH.
YEAH.
WH-WHAT'S...
...THE PROBLEM?!
THAT'S COPPING OUT.
BUT-!
ARE WE IN A POSITION TO BE WORRIED ABOUT *THAT?!*

KOFF
YOU'RE HURT, TOO.
DON'T MAKE IT ANY WORSE.
KOFF
I'LL BE FINE.
I'M NOT AS INJURED AS YOU THINK.
THEN SHOW ME YOUR HANDS.
I SAID, I'M FINE!
YANK
BISCUIT!
!!
...

SEE?!
I BET YOU CAN'T FEEL ANYTHING BUT *PAIN!*
I CAN STILL DO IT.
IT'S JUST ONE MORE TIME! GON, IT'S NO BIG DEAL!!
IT'S TOO MUCH!! GON, TELL HIM WHAT HE'S DOING TO HIMSELF!!
I KNEW ALL ALONG.
?!
I KNEW ABOUT...
...KILLUA'S HANDS.
TSEZGUERRA, I'M NOT STEPPING OUT.
I'M SORRY.
KILLUA HAS TO HOLD THE BALL.
I CAN'T DO THIS WITHOUT KILLUA.

I WON'T FEEL COM-FORTABLE...
...WITH HISOKA OR EVEN BISCUIT.
I CAN FOCUS ONLY ON HITTING THE BALL...
...BECAUSE KILLUA'S THE ONE HOLDING IT.
...
HEH.
DO YOU SEE NOW? GO AND GET YOUR REST.
...
ALL RIGHT.
GOOD LUCK.
GON...
I HOPE YOU HAVEN'T FORGOTTEN...
...WE HAVE TO GET THE BALL BACK FROM RAZOR FIRST!

I KNOW!
I SEE...
THAT WOULD BE FUN. ♥
LISTEN...
PSST
PSST
HMM.
I'M NOT SURE I CAN BE AS CONFIDENT...
REALLY?
I'D LOVE TO GIVE IT A TRY. ♥
HEH HEH
MAN.
YOU COME UP WITH THE MOST OUTRAGEOUS IDEAS.
I'M COUNTING ON YOU, KILLUA.
READY?
THE MATCH WILL RESUME!!

?!
SNAP
THE CONJURED GOONS...
...SUCKED AWAY?!
FSSSHHH

ALL THEIR AURA...
GOING BACK TO RAZOR...!!
M
M
V
M
HE RESTORED THE DISPERSED AURA. ♦
NOW WE'LL SEE HIS TRUE POWER. ♣
BRR
M

HEH... I DIDN'T THINK I'D USE THIS.
I HAVEN'T FELT THIS GOOD...
TOSS
...IN A LONG WHILE!!
?!!
HE TOSSED IT UP...
WAIT, IS THAT--

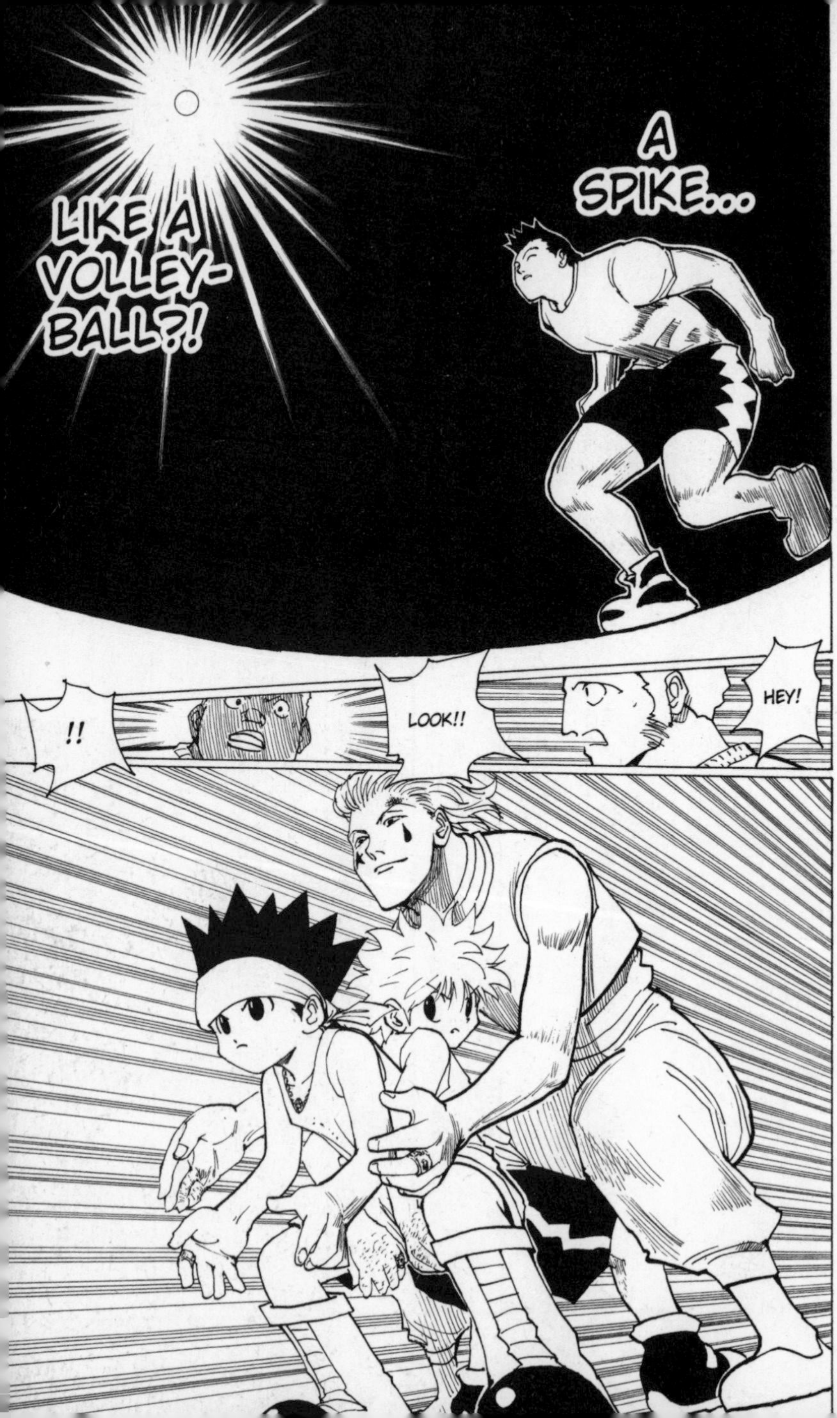
A SPIKE...
LIKE A VOLLEY-BALL?!
HEY!
LOOK!!
!!

46: GOLD DUST GIRL (A - 13)	A GIRL WHO SHEDS GOLD DUST FROM HER BODY--500 G [1 LB] OF GOLD CAN BE HARVESTED FROM HER DAILY BATH. VERY SHY, SHE RARELY LEAVES THE HOUSE.
47: SLEEPING GIRL (A - 11)	A GIRL WHO SLEEPS IN YOUR STEAD. YOU CAN BE ACTIVE FOR 24 HOURS WITHOUT SLEEPING WHILE SHE SLEEPS FOR YOU.
48: AROMATHERAPY GIRL (A - 15)	A GIRL WHO EMITS THE MOST COMFORTABLE AROMA FOR YOU. WHILE SHE'S BY YOUR SIDE, YOU WILL BE FREE OF STRESS.
49: MINIATURE MERMAID (B - 23)	A MERMAID SMALL ENOUGH TO FIT IN YOUR HAND. A COMFORTABLE LIVING ENVIRONMENT PUTS HER IN A GOOD MOOD, AND SHE WILL SING WITH HER BEAUTIFUL VOICE.
50: MINIATURE DINO (A - 11)	A DINOSAUR SMALL ENOUGH TO FIT IN YOUR HAND. THIS CREATURE PRODUCES A DIFFERENT SPECIES OF TINY DINOSAUR WITH EACH NEW GENERATION.
51: MINIATURE DRAGON (S - 10)	A DRAGON SMALL ENOUGH TO FIT IN YOUR HAND. IT WILL OBEY YOUR COMMANDS, AND WILL EVENTUALLY LEARN TO TALK IF RAISED WITH LOVE.
52: PEARL LOCUSTS (B - 30)	EACH OF THESE LOCUSTS HAS A PEARL IN ITS ABDOMEN. AN OUTBREAK OCCURS EVERY DOZEN OR SO YEARS.
53: KING WHITE STAG BEETLE (A - 30)	IT USES SPECIAL PHEROMONES TO LURE OTHER INSECTS TO BUILD A HUGE COLONY. IT LEAVES THE COLONY ONCE A DAY FOR AN EVENING STROLL.
54: MILLENNIUM BUTTERFLY (A - 25)	A LEGENDARY INSECT NAMED FROM THE FACT THAT THE FAMILY OF ANYONE WHO CAPTURES IT WILL PROSPER FOR GENERATIONS.

RAZOR...
...IS JUMP-SPIKING THE BALL!!
THE THREE OF THEM!
LOOK!!
THEY'RE AS ONE!!!
Chapter 167
Face-Off: Part 10

I KNOW WHAT YOU'RE TRYING TO DO!!
WHO WILL WIN?!
LET'S FIND OUT...

...THEIR STRATEGY!!!!
FOOM
GON STOPS THE BALL!!
HISOKA TRAPS IT!!
KILLUA BRACES!!

FSHHH
PLIP
PLOP

THEY DID IT!!
THEY STOPPED THE BALL!!!

WOOOOH
YES!
WOW!
WELL, I'LL BE...
KOFF
THEIR SKILLS PREVAILED OVER MY POWER.
THE CORE OF IT ALL WAS...
THAT BOY...
KILLUA!!
GON FOCUSED ALL HIS AURA IN HIS HANDS TO STOP THE BALL.
HE CAUGHT IT SQUARELY WITHOUT FEAR. IT TOOK COURAGE AND CONCENTRATION.
HISOKA ENVELOPED THE BALL WITH HIS ABILITY AT THE MOMENT OF IMPACT.
IT WOULD'VE BOUNCED AWAY WITHOUT QUICK ACTIVATION...

READ THIS WAY
AND KILLUA ...
BETWEEN THE TWO...
...HE WORKED AS BOTH CUSHION AND SUPPORT...
...BY DISTRIBUTING HIS AURA...!!
IF HE HAD INADEQUATE AURA IN HIS BODY, HE WOULDN'T BE EFFECTIVE AS A CUSHION...
...AND ALL THREE WOULD BE CRUSHED BY THE IMPACT OF THE BALL!!
ONE THE OTHER HAND, IF HE DIDN'T USE ENOUGH AURA IN HIS LEGS...
...ALL THREE OF THEM WOULD'VE BEEN FLUNG OUTSIDE THE COURT.
IT REQUIRED PRECISE DISTRIBUTION OF HIS AURA...
THE MARGIN OF ERROR WAS LESS THAN 1%!!
IN NEN COMBAT, BALANCING AURA DISTRIBUTION IS BOTH FUNDAMENTAL AND HARD TO MASTER.
NOTHING ELSE REQUIRES AS MUCH EXPERIENCE AND SKILL!!

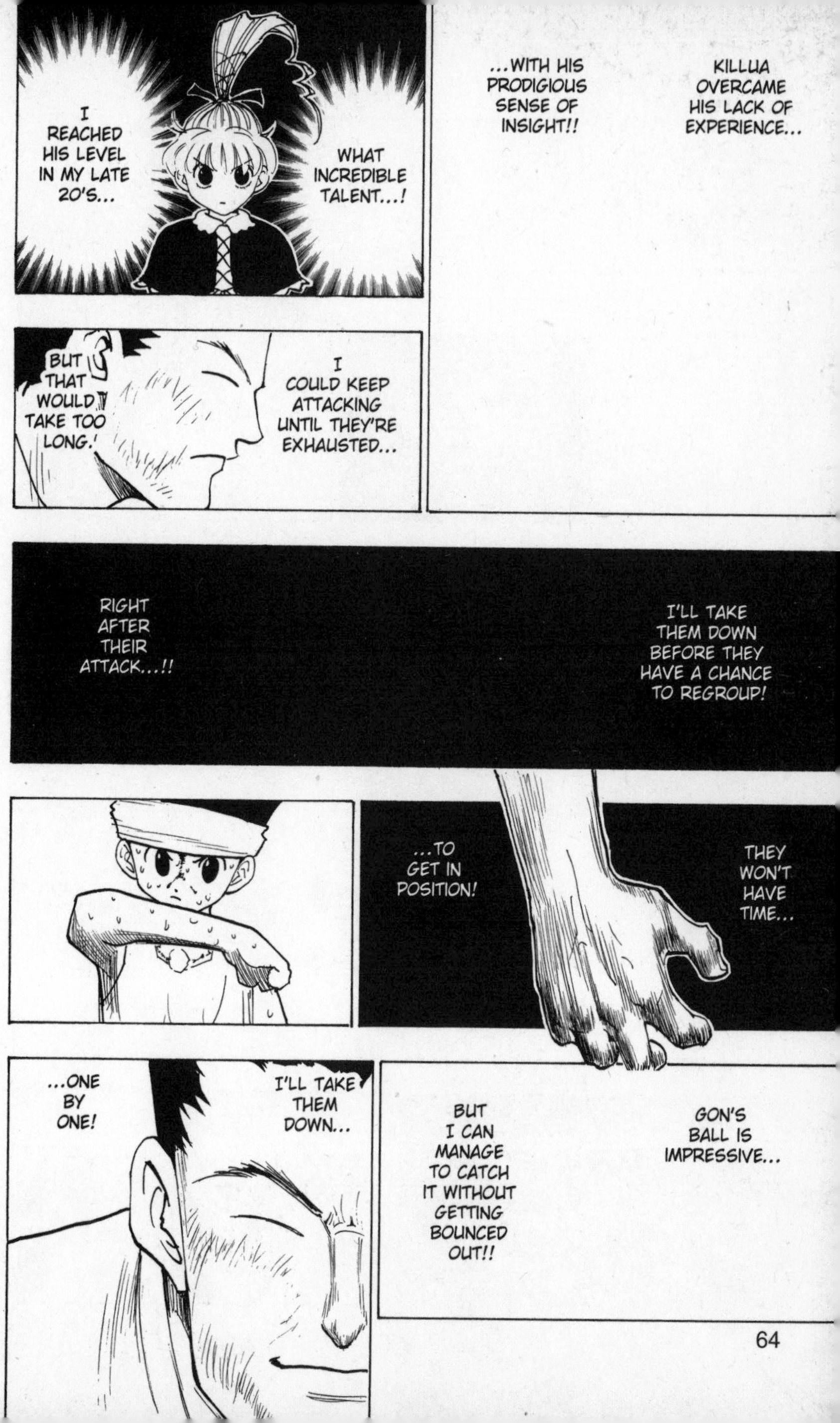
KILLUA OVERCAME HIS LACK OF EXPERIENCE...
...WITH HIS PRODIGIOUS SENSE OF INSIGHT!!
WHAT INCREDIBLE TALENT...!
I REACHED HIS LEVEL IN MY LATE 20'S...
I COULD KEEP ATTACKING UNTIL THEY'RE EXHAUSTED...
BUT THAT WOULD TAKE TOO LONG.
I'LL TAKE THEM DOWN BEFORE THEY HAVE A CHANCE TO REGROUP!
RIGHT AFTER THEIR ATTACK...!!
THEY WON'T HAVE TIME...
...TO GET IN POSITION!
GON'S BALL IS IMPRESSIVE...
BUT I CAN MANAGE TO CATCH IT WITHOUT GETTING BOUNCED OUT!!
I'LL TAKE THEM DOWN...
...ONE BY ONE!

MORE!!!
!!!

THAT LAST ONE...
...WASN'T HIS MAXIMUM...?!
...
MY GOD...
HE'S A MONSTER ...!!
GING...
YOU CAN BE PROUD.

THIS BOY...
...IS INDEED YOUR SON.
KILLUA.
I'LL GO AS HARD AS I CAN.
I'D SURE HOPE SO.
OR YOU'LL HEAR IT FROM ME.
SHOW ME...
...ROCK!

JAN!!
KEN!!!

ROCK
!!!!

55: REVENGE SHOP (A - 20)	REPORT YOUR GRUDGES TO THE MANAGER AND HE WILL RETALIATE FOR YOU IN PROPORTION TO YOUR GRIEVANCE. PAY EXTRA TO REQUEST A MORE SEVERE RETALIATION.
56: PERFECT MEMORY STUDIO (B - 25)	SPECIFY A TIME AND DATE TO GET A PICTURE OF YOURSELF IN THE PAST. YOU MAY ALSO REQUEST A SEQUENCE OF PHOTOGRAPHS.
57: HIDEOUT REALTOR (A - 11)	THE AGENT WILL BUILD A SECRET ROOM JUST FOR YOU AT A PLACE OF YOUR CHOOSING. HOWEVER, YOU MUST NOT TELL ANYONE ABOUT IT OR BRING ANYBODY TO IT.
58: SECRETS VIDEO RENTAL (A - 13)	RENT VIDEOS OF OTHER PEOPLE'S SECRETS. YOU MUST NOT SHOW THE VIDEO OR DISCUSS ITS CONTENTS WITH ANYONE.
59: INSTANT FOREIGN LANGUAGE SCHOOL (A - 20)	SPEND TIME STUDYING A LANGUAGE AT THIS SCHOOL, AND YOU WILL ACCRUE TIME ON A TIMER (INCLUDED). WHILE THE TIMER IS ACTIVATED AND COUNTING DOWN, YOU WILL BE FLUENT.
60: LONG LOST DELIVERY (B - 30)	CALL THE NUMBER AND DESCRIBE THE ITEM YOU LOST, AND IT WILL BE DELIVERED TO YOU THE NEXT DAY. IT MUST BE LOST FOR LONGER THAN A MONTH.
61: VENDING CHECK-UP (A - 20)	A FULL-BODY MEDICAL SCAN FOR JUST 500 J. HOWEVER, THE ONLY RESULTS ARE "ALL CLEAR" OR "ANOMALY DETECTED," IN WHICH CASE IT IS RECOMMENDED YOU SEE A DOCTOR.
62: CLUB "YOU RULE" (B - 20)	EVERYONE IN THE CLUB WILL DO YOUR BIDDING WHILE YOU ARE THERE. HOWEVER, ONE HOUR IN THE CLUB EQUALS A DAY OUTSIDE.
63: VIRTUAL RESTAURANT (B - 30)	YOU CAN ORDER ANY FOOD YOU WANT. YOU WILL FEEL FULL, BUT IT IS ONLY AN ILLUSION. YOU WILL BE GIVEN A MULTIVITAMIN AS YOU LEAVE.

Chapter 168
Face-Off: Part 11
THIS IS BEYOND MY EXPECTATIONS!!
I CAN STILL CATCH IT, BUT THE FORCE WILL PUSH ME OFF THE COURT.
CATCHING WON'T BE AN OPTION!!
BUT I CAN'T SHY AWAY!!

ANOTHER BUMP!!
HE'LL FALL VICTIM TO HISOKA AGAIN!!

COME!!!
OR WILL I?

THAT DEPENDS...
...ON THE DIRECTION...
...OF THE BUMP!!

GOTCHA!!!
WHAT THE...?!
HE BOUNCED IT BACK!!
GON, DUCK!!
YOU'LL STILL WIN!!
HE WON'T DUCK!!
THE PREVIOUS EXCHANGES SHOW THAT'S NOT HOW HE'D WANT TO WIN!!

THUD!!
HE PASSED OUT...!!
OF COURSE... HE USED UP EVERY LAST OUNCE OF HIS STRENGTH.
YOU CAN BE PROUD!!
YOU BEAT HIM, GON!!

NOT YET. ♥
DOOM
WHA-?
WHY?!
ONLY A FLAWLESS VICTORY WILL DO. ♣
THAT'S WHAT GON WANTS. ♥

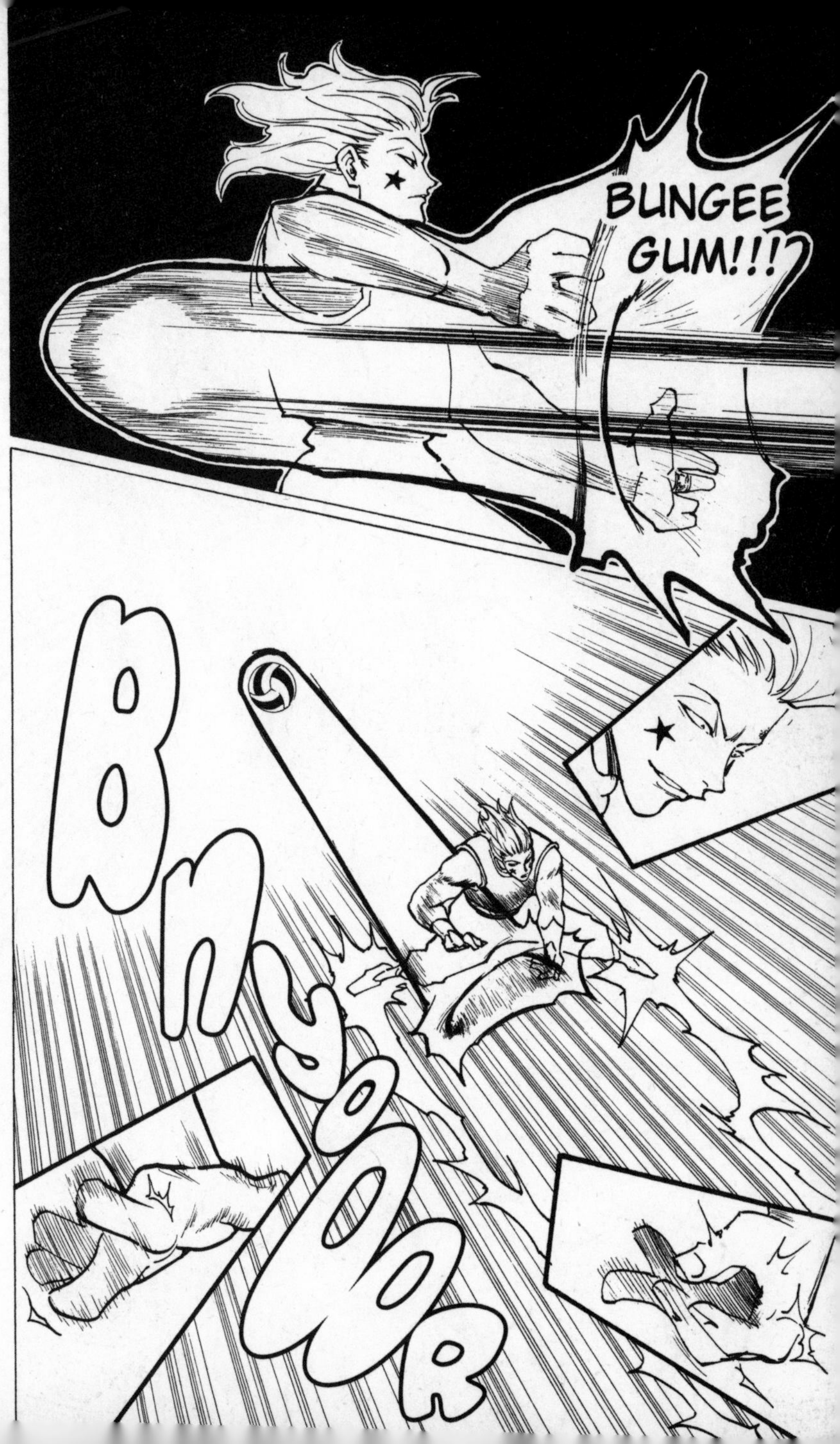
BUNGEE GUM!!!
BNYOOOOR

RUBBER SNAPS BACK!!
BYOING
WHOA!
HE BOUNCED IT BACK AGAIN!!
WELL, THIS IS FUN...!!
AN EXCHANGE OF VOLLEYS!!

WE'LL SEE WHO HOLDS OUT LONGEST!!
BM
SPLICH
?!!

IT'S STUCK!!
BUNGEE GUM HAS THE PROPERTIES...
...OF BOTH GUM AND RUBBER. ♣
AARRRRGG!
SKRKKKK

CATCHING THE BALL WHILE THE BODY IS TOUCHING OUTSIDE THE COURT IS NOT LEGAL!!
RAZOR IS OUT!!
BOTH HANDS, BUSTED. ♥
TA-DA!!
GON'S TEAM WINS THE GAME!!
HUH...?
OH YEAH!
YOU GUYS ARE AWESOME!!

WOOOH
WE WON!!
HUH...?
WHAT HAPPENED?!
POMM
A TOTAL DEFEAT.
SO HISOKA CLINCHED IT FOR US...
HE TOOK ALL THE JUICIEST PARTS.
WE ALL WORKED TOGETHER. ♣
IT WAS A TEAM VICTORY. ♥
YOU SOUND SO OUT OF CHARACTER.
♠

SHF
I LOSE.
WE'LL LEAVE TOWN, AS PROMISED.
OH YEAH.
WAS THAT OUR GOAL?
BUT FIRST...
I'LL ANSWER YOUR QUESTIONS...
...ABOUT GING.
!!

64: WITCH'S LOVE POTION (B - 30)	KISS A PILL AND HAVE YOUR INTENDED DRINK IT, AND HE OR SHE WILL FALL IN LOVE WITH YOU. ONE PILL LASTS ONE WEEK; ONE VIAL CONTAINS 500 PILLS.
65: WITCH'S REJUVENATION POTION (S - 10)	EACH PILL MAKES YOU PHYSICALLY YOUNGER BY ONE YEAR. YOU WILL RETAIN ALL KNOWLEDGE AND MEMORIES. BEWARE, AS YOU WILL DIE IF YOU TAKE MORE THAN YOUR AGE. ONE VIAL CONTAINS 100 PILLS.
66: WITCH'S DIET PILLS (B - 28)	EACH PILL MAKES YOU LOSE ONE KG. ONE VIAL CONTAINS 200 PILLS. BEWARE, AS YOU WILL DIE IF YOU TAKE MORE THAN YOU WEIGH.
67: DOYEN'S GROWTH PILLS (B - 30)	EACH PILL MAKES YOU GROW ONE CM TALLER. ONE VIAL CONTAINS 100 PILLS. NOT RECOMMENDED FOR PEOPLE UNDER 20 YEARS OF AGE.
68: DOYEN'S VIRILITY PILLS (A - 20)	A CERTAIN PART OF YOUR ANATOMY WILL GET VERY FRISKY. BOTH ENDURANCE AND FREQUENCY ARE ENHANCED. ONE VIAL CONTAINS 500 PILLS.
69: DOYEN'S HAIR RESTORER (B - 30)	LUXURIOUS HAIR WILL GROW WHEREVER IT IS APPLIED. USE GLOVES, OR HAIR WILL GROW ON FINGERS AND PALMS. ONE VIAL CONTAINS 200 ML (ENOUGH TO COVER TEN HEADS).
70: MAD SCIENTIST'S STEROIDS (A - 16)	GET ALL THE MUSCLES YOU WANT WITHOUT EXERCISE. YOU MUST DRINK A LITER A DAY FOR A WEEK, AND IT TASTES HORRIBLE. A SEVEN-BOX SET, WITH TEN ONE-L BOTTLES PER BOX.
71: MAD SCIENTIST'S PHEROMONES (A - 20)	SPRAY ON YOUR BODY TO ATTRACT THE OPPOSITE SEX. HOWEVER, YOU CANNOT ADJUST THE STRENGTH OF ITS EFFECT, SO BE CAREFUL AS IT MAY CAUSE A PROLIFERATION OF STALKERS.
72: MAD SCIENTIST'S PLASTIC SURGERY (A - 15)	SCAN A PICTURE OF THE FACE YOU WANT AND YOU WILL END UP AN EXACT LIKENESS. EACH SURGERY CARRIES A 5% CHANCE OF FAILURE, AND A 1% CHANCE THE MACHINE ITSELF WILL BREAK.

Chapter 169: Declaration of War

ABOUT GING...?!
YEAH.
LET'S STEP OVER THERE.
OWW!
GEEZ!
BOTH OF YOUR HANDS ARE A *MESS!!*
THEY MIGHT NEVER WORK RIGHT AGAIN...
ARE YOU LISTENING ?!
GLANCE

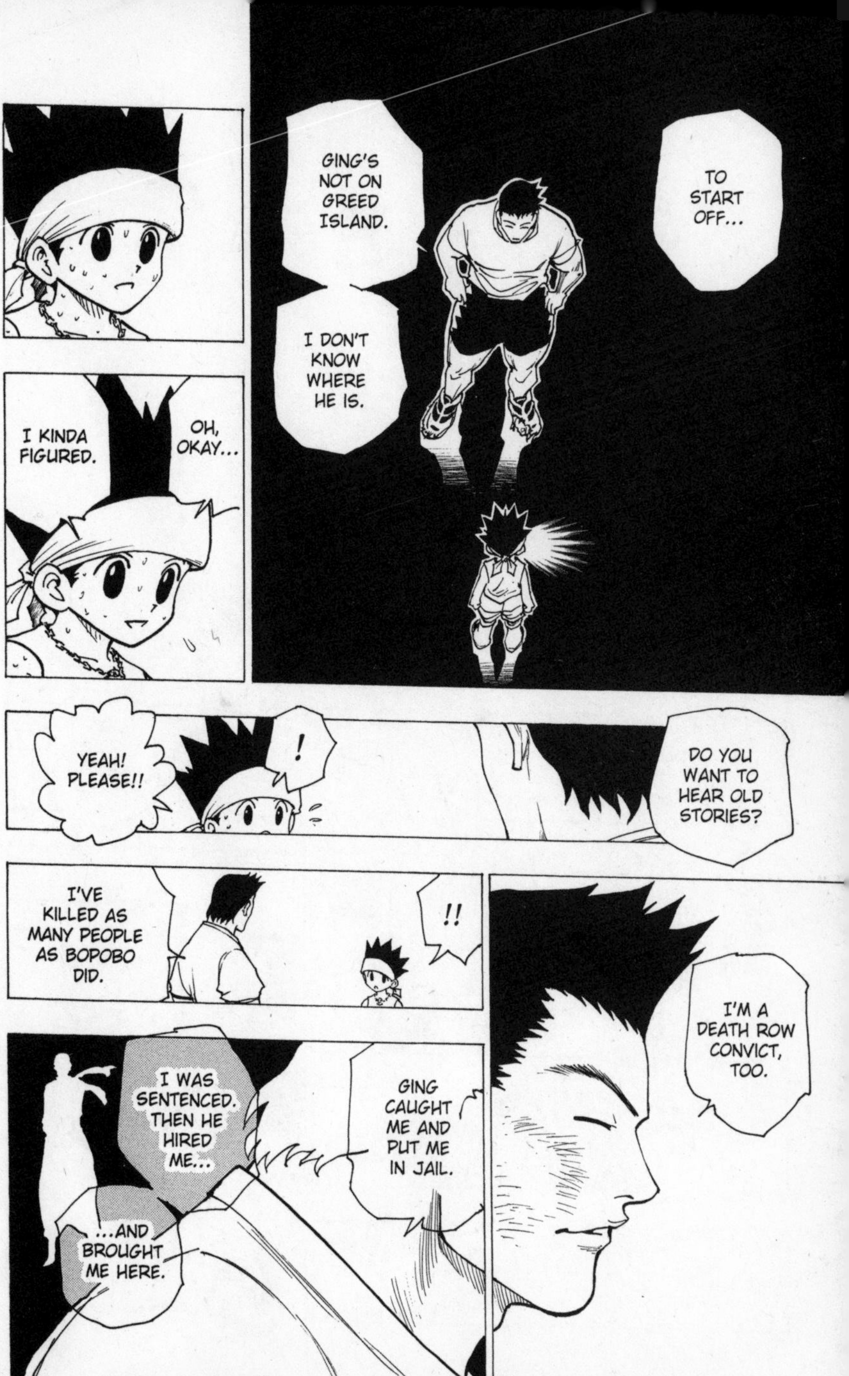
TO START OFF...
GING'S NOT ON GREED ISLAND.
I DON'T KNOW WHERE HE IS.
OH, OKAY...
I KINDA FIGURED.
DO YOU WANT TO HEAR OLD STORIES?
!
YEAH! PLEASE!!
I'M A DEATH ROW CONVICT, TOO.
!!
I'VE KILLED AS MANY PEOPLE AS BOPOBO DID.
GING CAUGHT ME AND PUT ME IN JAIL.
I WAS SENTENCED. THEN HE HIRED ME...
...AND BROUGHT ME HERE.

GING TAUGHT ME...
...THAT IF JUST ONE PERSON IN THE WHOLE WORLD BELIEVES IN YOU...
...YOU CAN BE REDEEMED.
ONE DAY...
...MY SON WILL COME TO GREED ISLAND.
DON'T HOLD BACK AGAINST HIM. GIVE HIM ALL YOU'VE GOT!
HEH...
YOU MEAN YOU WON'T MIND IF I KILL HIM?
DON'T UNDER-ESTIMATE HIM.
HE'S MY KID, AFTER ALL.
I'M COUNTING ON YOU!
RAZOR!!

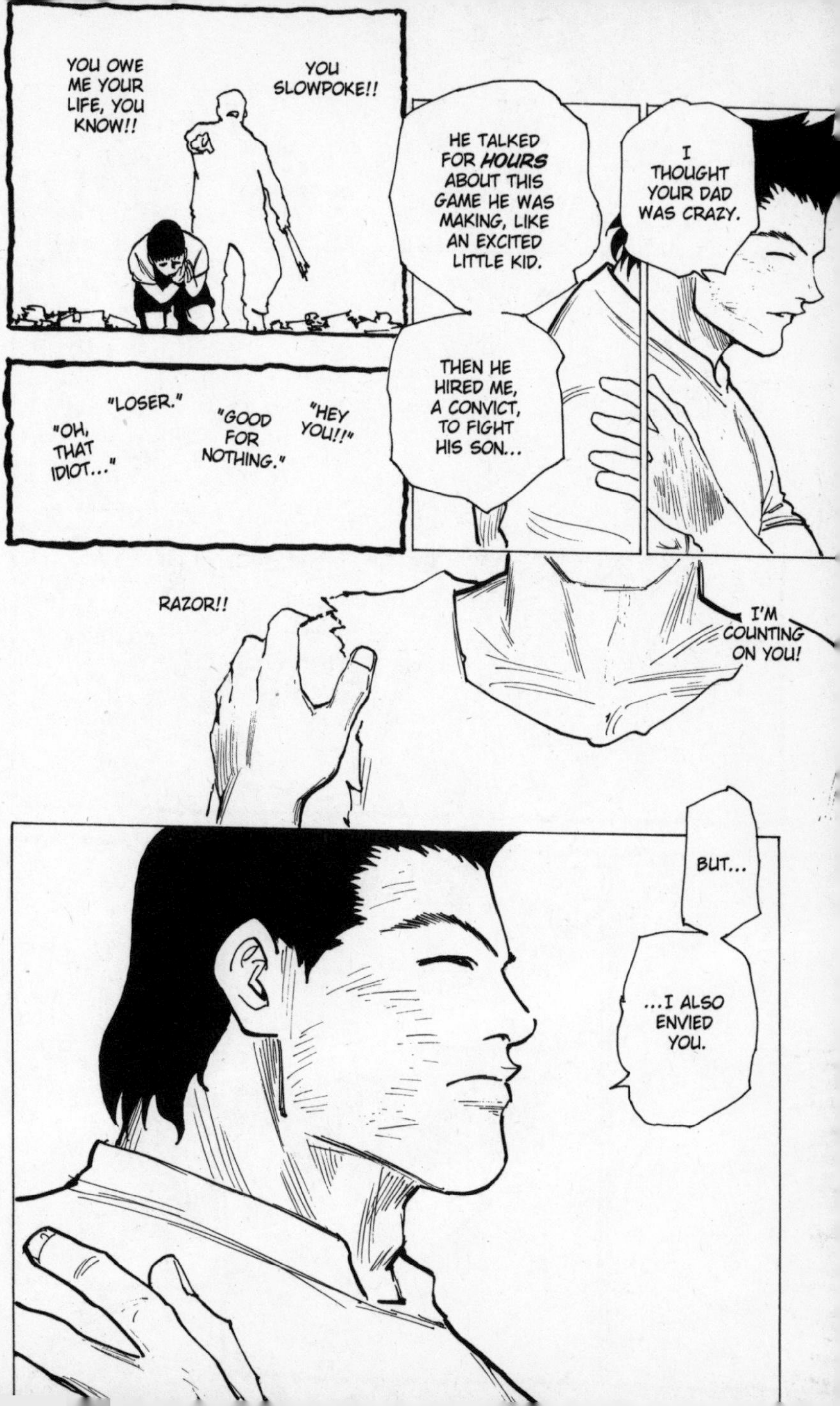
I THOUGHT YOUR DAD WAS CRAZY.
HE TALKED FOR **HOURS** ABOUT THIS GAME HE WAS MAKING, LIKE AN EXCITED LITTLE KID.
THEN HE HIRED ME, A CONVICT, TO FIGHT HIS SON...
YOU SLOWPOKE!!
YOU OWE ME YOUR LIFE, YOU KNOW!!
"HEY YOU!!"
"GOOD FOR NOTHING."
"LOSER."
"OH, THAT IDIOT..."
I'M COUNTING ON YOU!
RAZOR!!
BUT...
...I ALSO ENVIED YOU.

I FELT LIKE...
...I WAS CALLED BY NAME FOR THE FIRST TIME IN MY LIFE.
JUST AS GING BELIEVED IN YOU...
...AND ASKED ME TO DO THIS...
I BELIEVED IN YOU, TOO.
I SPARED NO EFFORT.
YEAH.
I COULDN'T HAVE DONE IT WITHOUT THE OTHERS.
YEAH. GOOD TEAMWORK.
GON.
I HOPE YOU SEE HIM!
THANKS!!

UP HERE.
THE ENTRANCE WAS RIGHT IN FRONT OF THEIR EYES ALL ALONG.
HERE IT IS.
A WINDOW ...?
YOU CAN SEE THE BEACH FROM HERE, BUT...
HOW DO YOU GET TO THE SEA CAVE FROM HERE?

TNK
CLIK
THERE'S A BUTTON...
WHRR
DIRECTLY UNDERNEATH THAT POINT...
...THERE'S AN UNDERWATER CAVE.
BUT THERE ISN'T ANY TREASURE.
I'M SORRY I LIED TO YOU.
THERE ISN'T?
IT'S SACRED GROUND, SO VERY FEW FISHERMEN ARE TOLD OF ITS LOCATION.
THE RUMORS ABOUT TREASURE TOOK ON A LIFE OF THEIR OWN.

THE PIRATES DIDN'T BELIEVE US.
MAYBE IF WE HAD TOLD THEM WHERE IT IS...BUT THEY WOULD'VE THOUGHT WE WERE LYING.
THEN NOBODY TOLD THEM WHERE POSEIDON'S CAVERN IS?
NO.
IT'S TOO SACRED.
THOSE WHO LIVE OFF THE OCEAN CANNOT DEFILE IT.
THAT'S WHAT THEY ALL SAID, BEFORE THEY DIED.
...
DON'T FORGET, THIS IS A STORY IN A GAME!
I CAN FINALLY SEE THE VIEW FROM HERE AGAIN.
THE RISING SUN... THE BOATS SAILING HOME... THE LIGHT DANCING ON THE WATER...
THIS IS THE GREATEST TREASURE OF THEM ALL...

OOH?!
2
PLOT OF BEACH
SS-3
THE ENTRANCE TO A CAVE CALLED "POSEIDON'S CAVERN." THE CAVE CHANGES ITS PATH AT EACH VISIT, CONFUSING INTRUDERS.
YES!! THE "PLOT OF BEACH" IS OURS!!
LET'S "CLONE" IT.
WE'LL TAKE THE COPIES.
YES.
YOU DESERVE TO TAKE THE ORIGINAL.
YOU SURE YOU DON'T WANT ANYTHING?
NOPE, I HAD ENOUGH FUN. ♥
I BETTER GO. ♠
WANNA GO WITH US?
TO KEEP AN EYE ON YOU.
YOU'RE GOING BACK TO COLLECTING CARDS, RIGHT? I'M NOT INTERESTED. ♦
"CONTACT" ME IF YOU NEED ME AGAIN. ♥
I'LL CAST "ACCOMPANY" OR "MAGNETIC FORCE." ♥

HEY!
HUH?
THAT BIG LIAR!
?
WE NEVER CAST "MAGNETIC FORCE" WHILE HE WAS HERE.
NO.
HE DID KNOW ABOUT SPELL CARDS BEFORE WE MET HIM.
OH!
♪
HE WAS HIDING SOMETHING!
KILLUA.
THERE ARE TWO KINDS OF LIARS: THOSE WHO LIE FOR A REASON, AND THOSE WHO DON'T.
YOU AND I ARE THE FORMER. HE'S THE LATTER.

OVER-ANALYZING WILL GET YOU MORE CONFUSED.
HMM.
GON.
WE NEED TO TALK.
WE DECIDED TO TEAM UP.
WANT TO JOIN US, TOO?
WE'LL HAVE TO HAVE A SHOWDOWN WITH GENTHRU.
BUT WE'RE AT A DISTINCT DISADVANTAGE.
EVEN WITHOUT MY INJURIES AND LACK OF PRACTICE, WE'D BE NO MATCH.
THAT'S THE IMPRESSION I GOT FROM YOUR DESCRIPTION OF HIS ABILITY.
HE CLEARLY LEARNED NEN TO KILL PEOPLE FROM THE OUTSET.
OUR APPROACHES TO COMBAT ARE FUNDAMENTALLY DIFFERENT.
FOOM!!
?!
A PLAYER HAS CAST "CONTACT" ON YOU.

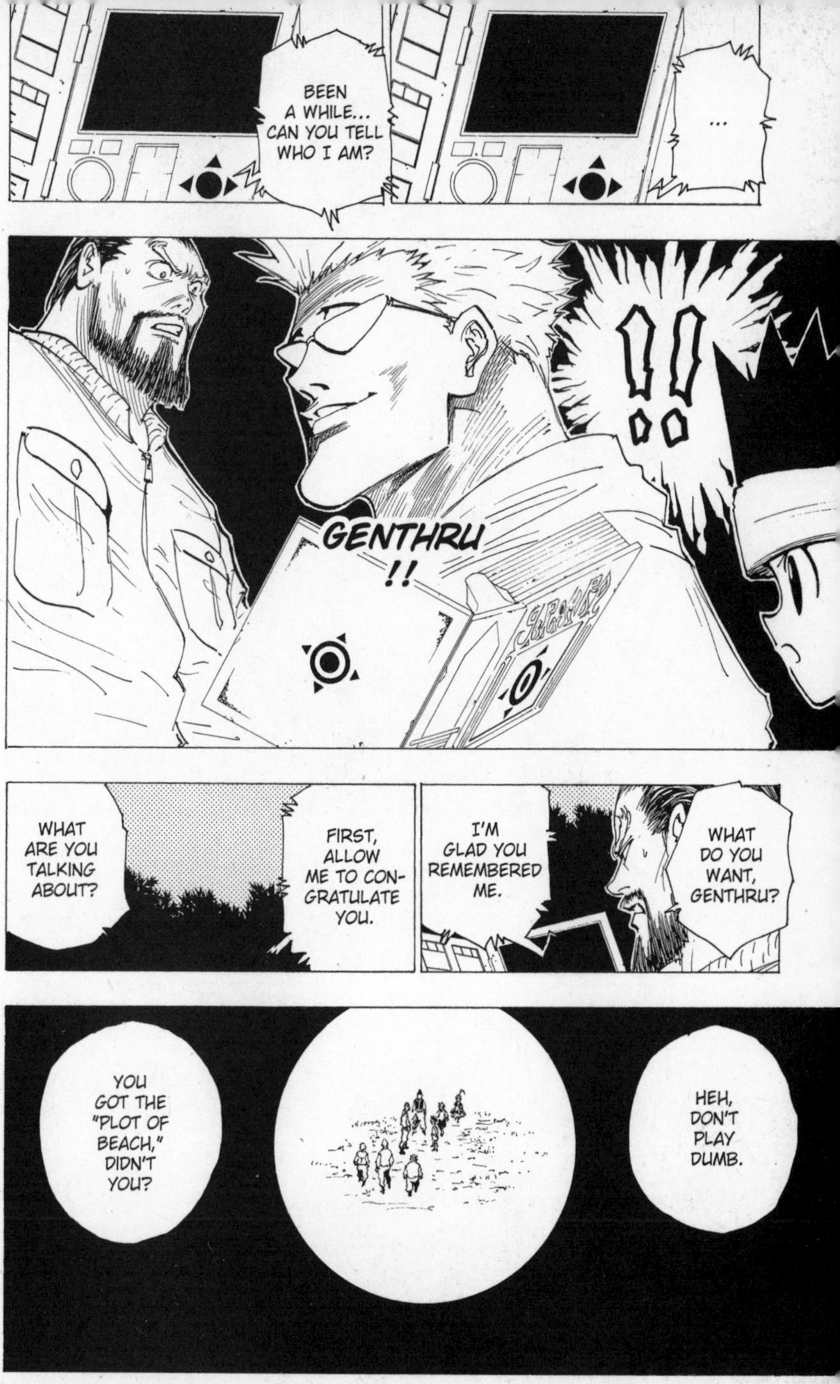
...
BEEN A WHILE... CAN YOU TELL WHO I AM?
GENTHRU !!
WHAT DO YOU WANT, GENTHRU?
I'M GLAD YOU REMEMBERED ME.
FIRST, ALLOW ME TO CONGRATULATE YOU.
WHAT ARE YOU TALKING ABOUT?
HEH, DON'T PLAY DUMB.
YOU GOT THE "PLOT OF BEACH," DIDN'T YOU?

WE JUST CAST "LIST" TO CONFIRM.
LET'S MAKE A DEAL.
WE'LL LET YOU LIVE...
...IF YOU HAND OVER THE "PLOT OF BEACH."
...
YEAH RIGHT!
HEH, DID YOU GET INJURED? YOUR VOICE SOUNDS FUNNY. OR ARE YOU BLUFFING?
WELL, IT'LL BE INTERESTING TO SEE IF YOU CAN BEAT US IN COMBAT.
IF YOU WANT TO TAKE THE DEAL, COME ALONE TO THE MASADORA GATE IN ONE HOUR.
IF YOU DON'T SHOW UP, WE'LL TAKE IT AS A DECLARATION OF WAR.
YOU CAN'T RUN OR HIDE...
WE HAVE PLENTY OF "ACCOMPANIES." HEH HEH HEH.
DAMN IT... DAMN IT!!
I KNEW THEY'D FIND OUT SOONER OR LATER, BUT... THAT WAS TOO FAST!!

ASTA, AMANA, MANHEIM.
NICK CUE, SOUHEIL, KAZSULE...
THEY WERE YOUR "GROUP OF 15"... RIGHT?
?
CHECK YOUR BINDERS.
THEY'RE NOT HERE ANYMORE... OR ANYWHERE AMONG THE LIVING.
WHA-
BOOK!!
EUGEN
YABIBI
MONTREUX
AMANA
MANHEIM
HANSE
WONG LI
TACKET
GENTHRU!!
...AND WHO ARE YOU?

I'M GON FREECSS!!
I'LL TAKE YOU ON!!
!!
GAH!
DING
A PLAYER HAS CAST "CONTACT" ON YOU.
IT'S ME, PHINKS... WE FOUND HIM.
WE'LL FLY RIGHT OVER.
HEH HEH

73: NIGHT JADE (A - 15)	A JEWEL "BLESSED" BY THE DEVIL. WHEN DANGER IS ABOUT TO BEFALL ITS OWNER, IT WILL DEFLECT IT TO SOMEONE ELSE.
74: SAGE'S AQUAMARINE (A - 15)	ITS OWNER WILL HAVE MANY INTELLIGENT FRIENDS AND KEEP THOSE FRIENDSHIPS FOR THEIR ENTIRE LIVES.
75: WILD LUCK ALEXANDRITE (A - 20)	ITS OWNER WILL GET TO HAVE ONCE-IN-A-LIFETIME EXPERIENCES, THOUGH YOU CANNOT CHOOSE WHETHER THEY'RE FOR BETTER OR FOR WORSE...
76: ROAMING RUBY (B - 30)	THE OWNER OF THIS RUBY WILL GAIN IMMENSE WEALTH, BUT WILL NEVER BE ABLE TO REMAIN IN THE SAME PLACE FOR MORE THAN A WEEK.
77: BEAUTY MAGNET EMERALD (S - 10)	SPECIALISTS OFFERING BEAUTY SERVICES WILL FLOCK TO ITS OWNER, WHO WILL SHINE WITH HERETOFORE UNRECOGNIZED BEAUTY.
78: LONELY SAPPHIRE (B - 30)	THE OWNER OF THIS SAPPHIRE WILL ACQUIRE VAST WEALTH, BUT IN EXCHANGE WILL SPEND A LIFETIME ALONE, FORSAKEN BY FRIENDS, FAMILY, AND SIGNIFICANT OTHERS.
79: RAINBOW DIAMOND (A - 20)	A DIAMOND THAT SHINES IN A RAINBOW OF COLORS. PROPOSE WITH THIS DIAMOND AND SHE IS GUARANTEED TO SAY "YES."
80: LEVITATION STONE (S - 7)	A STONE ABOUT ONE CARAT IN SIZE THAT LEVITATES. IT CAN LEVITATE ONE PERSON, AND RECEIVES ITS ENERGY FROM SUNLIGHT.
81: BLUE PLANET (SS - 5)	A UNIQUE BLUE JEWEL, ITS COMPOSITION DOES NOT CORRESPOND TO ANY KNOWN MINERAL, SO IT WAS GIVEN THIS NAME TO MEAN "A GIFT FROM SPACE."

Chapter 170
Three-Way Struggle: Part 1
GON... THE TEAM OF THREE KIDS?
I SAW YOU HAVE "WILD LUCK ALEXANDRITE."
YOU'LL BE NEXT, AFTER TSEZGUERRA. OR WILL YOU COME NOW TO HAND OVER YOUR CARDS?
YOU COME OVER!! WE'LL DEAL WITH YOU NOW!!
HAVE BEACH" TOO!!
LA LA LA LA LA LA!
TSEZGUERRA, TALK SOMEWHERE ELSE!!
TIME RAN OUT ALREADY.

WOULDN'T IT BE QUICKER TO GET "PLOT OF BEACH" FROM THE KIDS? I'M SURE THEY GOT A COPY, TOO...
BUT IT WOULD BE A "CLONED" COPY.
WE HAVE TO USE "PALADIN'S NECKLACE" IN CASE IT'S "FAKE," BUT THAT WILL ALSO CHANGE BACK A "CLONED" CARD.
THE KID WILL WILT ONCE HE SEES TSEZGUERRA SURRENDER.
HE'S COCKY NOW BECAUSE HE'S UNDER HIS PROTECTION.
WE DON'T WANT TO GIVE TSEZGUERRA TIME TO RECOVER.
HE'S A SINGLE-STAR PRO HUNTER! PLUS WE DON'T KNOW WHAT HIS ABILITY IS...
GENTHRU DOESN'T KNOW WHAT YOU CAN DO.
HE'S ASSUMING WE HAVE THE ORIGINAL "PLOT OF BEACH."
YOU KNOW FROM WEARING THAT NECKLACE...
IT FOILS A "FAKED" CARD DURING A TRADE...
...BUT ITS WEAKNESS IS THAT IT RUINS VALID CARDS MADE WITH "CLONE" AND "MIMIC."
THAT'S WHY HE'S AFTER THE ORIGINAL.
OUR "ORIGINAL."

WE'LL BUY AS MUCH TIME AS WE CAN.
HEAL YOUR INJURIES IN THE MEAN-TIME.
!
WE CAN'T AVOID A FIGHT IF WE WANT TO WIN!
AND YOU'RE THE ONLY ONES WITH A CHANCE TO BEAT HIM.
AS FOR *YOU*, GON...
WHAT YOU JUST DID WAS SELFISH AND FOOLISH!!
IF THEY HAD ACTUALLY COME HERE LIKE YOU SUGGESTED, WHAT WOULD'VE HAPPENED TO KILLUA?!
YOU USED UP YOUR AURA, AND YOU WON'T EVEN BE ABLE TO *MOVE* UNTIL TOMORROW!!
YOU IMPULSIVELY EXPOSED NOT ONLY YOURSELF, BUT ALSO YOUR FRIENDS TO DANGER!!
...
...
I'M SORRY...

ANYWAY ...
NOW IT DEPENDS ON OUR SPELLS...!
IF WE CAN STAVE OFF THEIR PURSUIT...
...WE'LL BE ABLE TO BUY SOME TIME.
BUT IF *TOO* MUCH TIME PASSES...
...THEY MIGHT RECONSIDER AND TARGET YOU INSTEAD.
WE CAN HOLD THEM OFF FOR A WEEK, *IF* THAT...!
NO MORE.
JUST ONE WEEK... IT'S TOO SHORT...!!
NO, EVEN *THAT'S* BEING OPTIMISTIC. THERE'S NO BASIS FOR THIS ESTIMATE. THEY MIGHT COME AFTER US SOONER.
HOLD ON. WHAT ABOUT OUR EARLIER DISCUSSION?
I'M TEAMING UP WITH TSEZGUERRA— WHAT ABOUT YOU?

THIS IS ALL ASSUMING WE HAVE AN ALLIANCE, RIGHT?
NO, WAIT.
THE SITUATION HAS CHANGED.
THERE ARE NOW FEW MERITS TO FORMING AN ALLIANCE.
THEY'VE FOUND OUT THAT WE'VE BEEN WORKING TOGETHER.
ANY OPTIONS WE HAD FOR YOU TO SURPRISE-ATTACK WHILE WE DISTRACT THEM ARE GONE.
THE CARDS THEY WANT ARE NOS. 2 AND 75.
IT'S DANGEROUS TO BE HOLDING BOTH THESE ORIGINAL CARDS IN ONE PARTY.
THE CONS OUTWEIGH THE PROS!
...
SO OUR OFFER TO BUY TIME...
...IS BASED ON A *TRADE*, NOT AN ALLIANCE.
A TRADE?

WE'LL BUY YOU *THREE WEEKS!!*
IF WE SUCCEED, WILL YOU GIVE US NO. 75: "WILD LUCK ALEXANDRITE"?
?!
YOU JUST SAID ONE WEEK'S THE LIMIT.
THAT'S IF WE'RE ONLY TRYING TO EVADE THEM.
IF WE GO ON THE OFFENSIVE...
...THE RISKS WILL INCREASE, BUT WE'LL KEEP THEIR ATTENTION ON *US!*
WE CAN TURN IT INTO A WAR OF ATTRITION IF NEED BE.
I SEE.
BUT WE CAN TELL YOU *HOW* TO GET NO. 75, IN EXCHANGE FOR SOME CARDS.
WE KNOW HOW TO GET IT.
BUT THE FIVE OF US, GOREINU INCLUDED, HAVE FEW EMPTY SLOTS IN OUR BINDERS.
IT'S IMPOSSIBLE FOR US TO GIVE THE VILLAGERS ALL OUR CARDS.

THREE WEEKS...
NOT ENOUGH TIME FOR KILLUA'S HANDS TO HEAL, MUCH LESS COME *CLOSE* TO GENTHRU IN POWER.
SO YOU WANT US TO COME UP WITH A PLAN.
YES.
FORM A STRATEGY IN THREE WEEKS...
...TO LURE THEM INTO A SITUATION WHERE...
...YOU CAN GUARANTEE YOURSELVES THE UPPER HAND!!
DEAL!
GOOD...! WE'LL BE STALLING GENTHRU FOR THREE WEEKS, STARTING TODAY!
DON'T FORGET, GON.
THEY'VE KILLED MORE THAN 50 PLAYERS SO FAR.
IF YOU WANT TO CLEAR THE GAME... YOU MUST *FIGHT!*

DOOM!!
THREE WEEKS...
IT *IS* TOO SHORT.
KILLUA, FOCUS ON *HEALING*.
AND YOU'RE IN CHARGE OF FORMING A STRATEGY.
GON, YOU PRACTICE WITH ME!!
AT *MINIMUM* YOU MUST BE ABLE TO AVOID HIS LITTLE FLOWER.
RIGHT!
ZINK!!

FSHHHH
WHERE'S YOUR FRIEND?
MACHI AND NOBUNAGA ARE TAILING.
FOLLOW THIS THREAD.
WE'LL LEAVE YOU TO NEGOTIATE WITH THE EXORCIST.

WE'LL PAY WHATEVER HE ASKS.
JUST GET HIM TO DO THE JOB.
I KNOW. ♠
OR ELSE I WON'T BE ABLE TO FIGHT CHROLLO. ♣
THAT'S HIM.
HOW'D YOU FIND HIM?
AS IF WE'D TELL YOU, IDIOT.

YOU IN THE SHADOWS...
...WAS IT *YOUR* ABILITY?
...
HEH HEH, I JUST HAD A *VERY* FUN BATTLE. ♥
THE RUSH HAS LEFT ME... *SEN-SITIZED.*
TCH.
YOU'RE A FREAK...!
YOU'RE NOT EVEN USING NEN.
TO SOOTHE MY AROUSAL...
...I WOULDN'T MIND RAVAGING SOMEONE I DON'T KNOW, SEE?
FEH!
COME OUT!!

WAS MY ZETSU...
...NOT GOOD ENOUGH?
IT WAS PERFECT.
HE'S ABNORMAL, THAT'S ALL.
HE'S MEMBER NO. 4. YOUR REPLACEMENT.
MY NAME IS KALLUTO.
BUT IT WAS MY ABILITY.
I CAN'T TELL YOU HOW I DID IT.
OH. ♦
YOU LOOK TASTY, TOO. ♥
...
CAREFUL.
HE'LL GO AFTER ANYTHING.

HISOKA.
MAKE THIS WORK.
QUIT HARPING ON IT. ♠
I'LL MAKE IT WORK, FOR *MY OWN SAKE*. ♦
YOU'RE SERIOUSLY GOING TO FIGHT CHROLLO?
OF COURSE. ♥
DO YOU HAVE A PREFERENCE WHO SURVIVES, MACHI?
STUPID QUESTION.
YOU CAN DROP DEAD WHEN YOUR JOB IS DONE.
IF I END UP KILLING CHROLLO...?
NOT LIKELY.
BUT I'LL GIVE YOU AN ANSWER.
I'LL CHASE YOU TO THE ENDS OF THE EARTH...
...AND KILL YOU.
SOUNDS NICE. ♦

BLOOP
BLOOP
WE WANT "ANGEL'S BREATH," WHICH GENTHRU IS MONOPOLIZING!!
WE HAVE TO MAKE THEM USE ONE UP, OR WE CAN NEVER CONVERT OUR EXCHANGE VOUCHER.
IDEALLY, WE'D STEAL IT...
BUT THE PROBABILITY WITH "LEVY" IS LOW.
OTHER METHODS ARE HIGH-RISK, WITH LOW CHANCE OF SUCCESS.
THAT'S WHERE GON'S TEAM COMES IN.
YES.
WHETHER THEY WIN OR NOT...
...IT'S LIKELY THEY'LL INJURE ONE OF GENTHRU'S TEAM.
IF THEY USE EVEN *ONE* OF THEIR "ANGEL'S BREATHS"...
...OUR VOUCHER WILL INSTANTLY TRANSFORM INTO "ANGEL'S BREATH"!!
102
EXCHANGE VOUCHER
SS-150
A VOUCHER THAT CAN BE EXCHANGED WITH "ANGEL'S BREATH." THIS IS AVAILABLE ONLY WHEN "ANGEL'S BREATH" IS MAXED OUT.
THEN...
ALL WE'LL HAVE LEFT IS "WILD LUCK ALEXANDRITE"!!

THOUGH IT'S THE OTHER WAY AROUND.
WE'LL GET "WILD LUCK ALEXANDRITE" *FIRST* BY BUYING THREE WEEKS' TIME.
GON WILL FIGHT GENTHRU AFTER-WARDS.
WHAT IF THEY BEAT GON'S TEAM WITHOUT USING "ANGEL'S BREATH"...?
IT'LL DEPEND ON THE NO. 0 EVENT...LET'S FOCUS ON THIS MISSION FOR NOW.
IT'S TIME.
LET'S GO.

82: STAFF OF JUDGMENT (A - 15)	RAISE THIS STAFF IN THE AIR WHILE CALLING OUT THE NAME OF SOMEONE YOU WANT TO PUNISH, AND CALAMITY WILL BEFALL THE ONE OF YOU WHO HAS COMMITTED MORE BAD DEEDS, THE TARGET OR YOURSELF.
83: SWORD OF TRUTH (B - 22)	SPLITS IN TWO ANYTHING AND ANYONE DECEITFUL. IN TRIALS, IT'S A CRIMINAL'S WORST NIGHTMARE. THE SWORD WILL SHATTER WHEN USED TO CUT SOMETHING TRUE, BUT WILL REGENERATE IF STORED IN ITS SCABBARD FOR ONE DAY.
84: PALADIN'S NECKLACE (D - 60)	A PLAYER WEARING THIS WILL REFLECT CURSES CAST UPON HIM, AND BE ABLE TO UNDO CURSES PLACED ON CARDS HE TOUCHES.
85: SCAPEGOAT/SACRIFICE ARMOR (S - 8)	RENDERS INEFFECTIVE ANY ATTACK BY A WEAPON REVERTED FROM A CARD. BEWARE, AS IT WILL RANDOMLY BREAK SOMETIME WITHIN THE FIRST 100 ATTACKS.
86: QUIVER OF FRUSTRATION (A - 11)	YOU WILL BE ABLE TO CAST AS MANY "LEAVES" AS YOU HAVE ARROWS. IT COMES WITH 10 ARROWS, AND ONE WILL BE USED EACH TIME YOU CAST "LEAVE."
87: SHIELD OF FAITH (S - 15)	THE SPELLS "RELEGATE," "ORIGIN," "DRIFT," AND "COLLISION" WILL BE RENDERED INEFFECTIVE WITHIN A RADIUS OF 20 M OF THE PLAYER ARMED WITH THIS SHIELD.
88: ETERNAL HAMMER (A - 15)	ANYONE HIT WITH THIS HAMMER WILL BE AFFLICTED WITH ONE RANDOM ATTACK SPELL, AND CANNOT DEFEND HIM OR HERSELF WITH A DEFENSIVE SPELL. HOWEVER, IT WILL NOT WORK ON SOMEONE USING "FORTRESS" OR "PALADIN'S NECKLACE."
89: TAX COLLECTOR'S GAUNTLET (A - 20)	GRANTS YOU THE ABILITY TO CAST "LEVY." HOWEVER, IT WILL DESTROY ONE RANDOM SPECIFIED SLOT CARD FROM YOUR BINDER EVERY TIME. (YOU CANNOT CAST IT IF YOUR SPECIFIED SLOTS ARE EMPTY.)
90: MEMORY HELMET (A - 20)	YOU WILL NEVER FORGET THINGS YOU SEE OR HEAR WHILE WEARING THIS HELMET. UNFORTUNATELY, IT'S EXTREMELY LARGE AND HEAVY.

Chapter 170
Three-Way Struggle: Part 2

WE'LL FIGHT.
LEAP
"LEVY" ON!!
"ACCOMPANY" ON!!
TO MASADORA!!

SHOOOOM
ZUNK
BOOK!
CHECK YOUR CARDS.
THEY ONLY GOT JUNK CARDS IN MY FREE SLOTS.
SAME HERE.
ME TOO.
THAT SETTLES IT.
LET'S TAKE THEIR CARDS AND KILL THEM.
IT'LL BE TOUGH.
HUH?
I DON'T KNOW WHAT HAPPENED, BUT...
HE SEEMED FULLY COMMITTED ...!!

SIX "ACCOMPANIES," NINE "DRAWBRIDGES," TWO "MAGNETIC FORCES," AND 24 "RETURNS"...
THAT'S ALL THE MONEY I HAD.
O.K., SEE YOU IN THREE DAYS.
RAISE MONEY TO BUY MORE CARDS.
GOT IT.
DO YOU THINK GENTHRU WILL COME AFTER US?
NOT YET.
WE HAVE TWICE AS MANY "ACCOMPANIES" AS THEY DO.
THAT'S EASY TO FIND OUT WITH 96: "CLAIRVOYANT SNAKE."
I'LL SHOW YOU, GENTHRU...
...WHAT A SINGLE-STAR HUNTER CAN DO...!!

UNH!
GUH!
GRAB
GYO!!

TOO SLOW!!
REACT AS SOON AS THE SKIN FEELS A TOUCH, NOT WHEN THE MIND CATCHES UP!!!
RIGHT!
TEN-MINUTE BREAK!
WE'LL PRACTICE EMISSION NEXT.
OKAY!
HIS STAMINA IS KEEPING UP.
BUT WE'LL USE UP MOST OF THE TIME ON DEFENSIVE PRACTICE ALONE.
TO BE ABLE TO FIGHT...
...WE NEED ANOTHER WEAPON...!!

EMISSION TRAINING, LEVEL TWO.
FLOATING HAND.
DO A HAND-STAND...
DON'T MOVE.
ONLY BY EMITTING AURA...
FASH
!!
PROPEL YOUR BODY OFF THE GROUND!!
FOOM

THERE.
YOU PASS WHEN YOU CAN LAUNCH YOURSELF THIS MUCH.
HM.
SHEEN
HAH !!!!

PUFF
KEEP GOING AS LONG AS YOU CAN MAINTAIN THE HAND-STAND.
RIGHT ...!
HAH!
PUFF...
PUFF...
YAH!!!
HOW ARE YOUR HANDS?
IT HURTS IF I MOVE A TINY BIT.
THEY'RE NOT GETTING BETTER AT ALL.
THAT EXERCISE IS...
...MUCH HARDER FOR BEING ONLY ONE LEVEL UP.
YAH!
TAH!
WELL, I'D THINK SO. IT'S ACTUALLY FOR LEVEL *FIVE.*
HMPH!
FIVE?!

YOU WANT HIM TO JUMP AHEAD?
IT'S A GAMBLE.
HAH!
UNH!
IF HE FAILS TO LEARN IT...
...THE THREE WEEKS WILL BE A WASTE.
BWONNG
HE'D PROBABLY GET TO LEVEL THREE IF WE DID IT STEP BY STEP...
BUT THAT WON'T BE USEFUL ENOUGH IN COMBAT.
HE'D NEED TO BE ABLE TO KNOCK SOMEONE BACK A DOZEN FEET WITH A DIRECT HIT.
ANYTHING LESS WON'T BE EFFECTIVE AS A WEAPON.
AND THAT'S LEVEL FIVE...
HAH!
BUT IT WON'T BE A FINISHING BLOW EVEN IF HE GOT TO LEVEL FIVE...
NO.
BUT IT BROADENS OUR TACTICAL OPTIONS.
WHAT'S YOUR ABILITY?
KNOWING IT WOULD MAKE IT EASIER TO PLAN.

!!
ALLOW ME TO INTRODUCE...
...COOKIE, THE MAGICAL MASSEUSE.

HER VARIOUS MASSAGE TECHNIQUES ARE CARESSES OF SHEER BLISS!! THEY MELT AWAY FAT DEPOSITS AND MAKE YOU FEEL HEAVENLY!
AURA IS TRANSMUTED INTO SPECIAL LOTION, SMOOTHING AND REJUVENATING YOUR SKIN!!
HER SHIATSU MASSAGE MAKES YOU BEAUTIFUL FROM THE INSIDE OUT!! IT IMPROVES CIRCULATION, AND RELIEVES CONSTIPATION AND MUSCLE STIFFNESS!!
THAT'S IT?
NOT AT ALL!!
SWEDISH MASSAGE, ROLLING MASSAGE, AND MORE!
WHAT THE HELL!! YOU'RE FREAKIN' USELESS!!
ARE YOU KIDDING?! IT'S THE BEST ABILITY EVER!

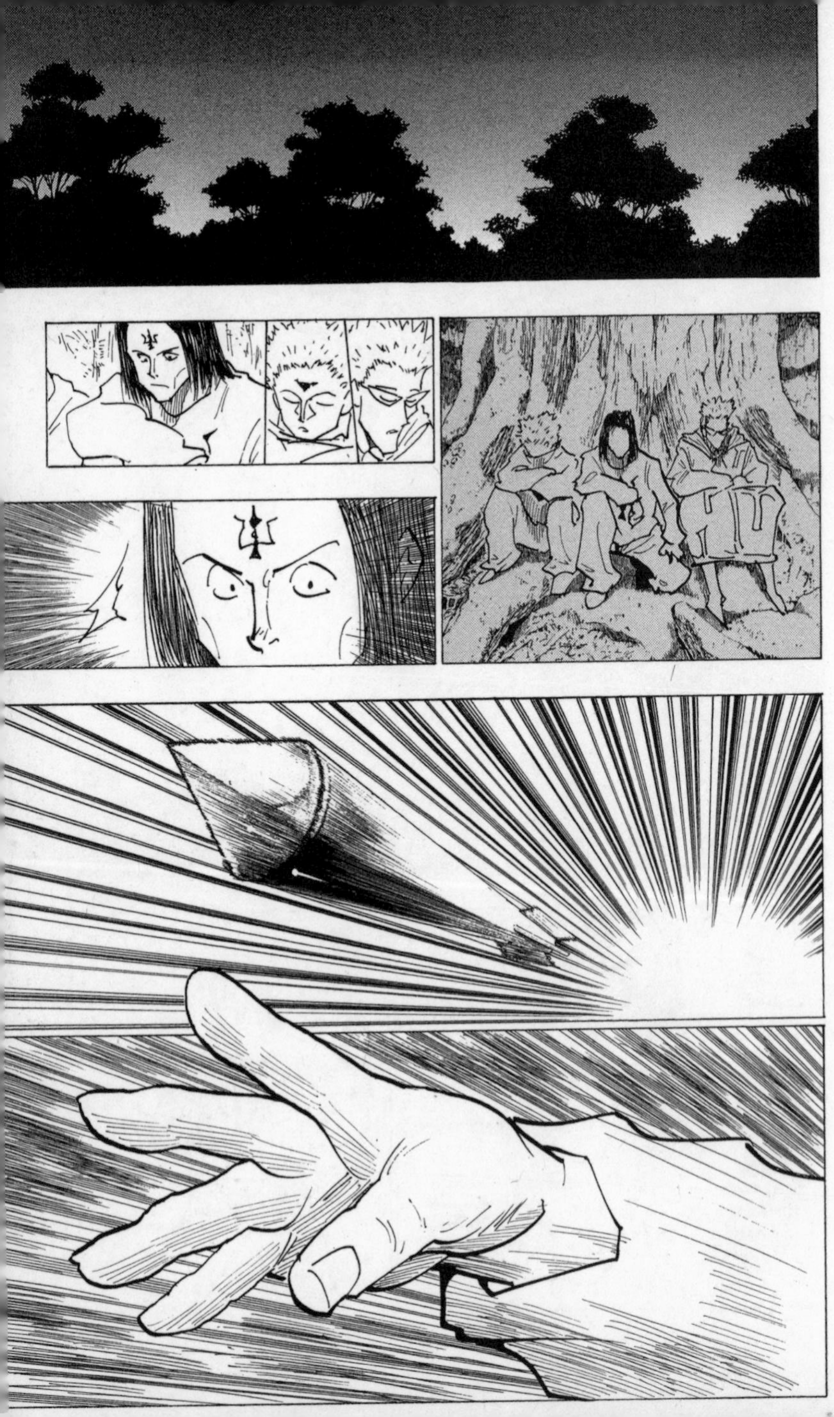

WHP
HEY!
IS IT THEM?!
DON'T BOTHER.
"RETURN" ON, TO SOUFRABI!
FSH
ARGH!
KRAK
DAMN!
THEY'RE GETTING MORE AND MORE BRAZEN.
HE CLEARLY AIMED TO KILL.
THAT'S NOT THE PROBLEM.
HOW DO THEY KNOW WHERE WE ARE?

READ THIS WAY

91: PLASTIC KING (A - 20)	RECOMBINE THE PARTS OF THIS 1:1 SCALE MODEL KIT TO BUILD ANY KIND OF VEHICLE. FULLY FUNCTIONAL, FUEL NOT INCLUDED.
92: SWAP TICKET (S - 7)	RIP THE TICKET AND GIVE IT TO SOMEONE YOU WANT TO SWITCH WITH, AND YOU CAN LIVE HIS LIFE FOR 24 HOURS. BOOK OF 1000.
93: BOOK OF LIFE (B - 28)	AN ENCYCLOPEDIA OF EVERYONE WHO'S BEEN IN YOUR LIFE SINCE YOUR BIRTH, WITH RECORDS OF CONVERSATIONS AND MEMORABLE INCIDENTS. IT MAY END UP BEING TENS OF THOUSANDS OF PAGES LONG.
94: BANDIT'S BLADE (S - 10)	A SUCCESSFUL ATTACK WITH THIS WEAPON WILL CAST "MUG," "PICKPOCKET," OR "THIEF" ON THE TARGET. NOT EFFECTIVE ON SOMEONE USING "FORTRESS" OR "PALADIN'S NECKLACE."
95: SECRET CAPE (A - 20)	YOU WILL BE UNDER THE EFFECT OF "BLACKOUT CURTAIN" WHILE WEARING THIS CAPE.
96: CLAIRVOYANT SNAKE (A - 12)	FEED IT A CARD RANK C OR ABOVE, AND IT WILL SPIT UP A "CLAIRVOYANCE."
97: 3-D CAMERA (A - 20)	PICTURES TAKEN WITH THIS WILL BE DEVELOPED AS 3-D OBJECTS, WITH ALL TEXTURES REPRODUCED. MAKE ENLARGEMENTS AS NEEDED.
98: SILVER DOG (S - 8)	AN ENDANGERED SPECIES WITH SILVER FUR. MIX 5 G OF GOLD INTO ITS FOOD EVERY DAY AND IT WILL EXCRETE ONE KG OF SOLID SILVER FECES.
99: PANDA MAID (S - 8)	AN ENDANGERED SPECIES. VERY NEAT AND LOVES TO COOK, AND EACH HAS A HOBBY SUCH AS SEWING OR GARDENING. THEY ARE EXCELLENT AT TAKING CARE OF HUMAN CHILDREN.

BLOOP
BLOOP
Chapter 170
Three-Way Struggle: Part 3
I CAN'T GET A "LEAVE" FOR THE LIFE OF ME.
SIGH
HEY.

UNH.
GUH...
PLEASE... SPARE ME...
NO MORE...
SHOW US YOUR BINDER.
OKAY THEN...
SET A "PEEK" INTO HIS BINDER...
CLIK
OOH.
SCORE ONE "ACCOMPANY"!
TAKE ANY RANK C CARDS, TOO.
HE HASN'T MET HIM.
THEN HE'S INNOCENT.

HEY.
EVER HEARD OF THE BOMBER?
YES... RUMORS...
GOOD.
WE'RE THEM.
BOM!!
I JUST SET A BOMB ON YOUR BODY! I CAN DETONATE IT WHENEVER I WANT.
IF YOU DON'T WANT TO DIE, BRING US THE CARDS WE NEED.
ONE "MAGNETIC FORCE" OR TWO "ACCOMPANIES"!
THEN WE'LL DISARM THE BOMB.
"CONTACT" US WHEN YOU GET THE CARDS.
GOT IT?
Y-YES.
GOOD LUCK!
OKAY, NEXT.
SHF

SHOW US YOUR BINDER.
SCORE ANOTHER "ACCOMPANY"!
SET THE "PEEK" IN THE BINDER...
HM?
OOH!
TSEZGUERRA
BOOOM
...
OH NO!
TOO BAD!!
BUSTED!!
HUH?
WH-WHAT'S WRONG?

BOOM!!
PUNISH ALL SUSPECTS!!
FSHH
OKAY, NEXT.
OH MAN...
I CAN'T BELIEVE THEM...!!

THEY'RE STAKING OUT THE SPELL CARD SHOP.
AND ATTACKING EVERY PLAYER WHO BUYS SPELL CARDS.
THIS IS JUST A GUESS, BUT...
I'M PRETTY SURE I'M RIGHT.
THEY'VE REALIZED THAT SOMEONE...
...HAS BEEN SUPPLYING CARDS TO YOU GUYS.
TO FIND ME, THEY'RE CHECKING THE BINDERS OF EVERYONE WHO ENTERS THE SHOP...
...AND THEN KILLING ANYONE WHO'S EVER MET YOU IN THE GAME. NO DISCUSSION...!!
THEY'RE ALSO TAKING CARDS FROM THEM. PROBABLY "ACCOMPANY" AND "MAGNETIC FORCE."
THEY'RE ALSO FORCING PLAYERS THEY RELEASE TO GET THEM MORE CARDS.
THEY'RE ELIMINATING SUSPECTS, COLLECTING CARDS, AND CUTTING OFF YOUR SUPPLY!!
KILLING THREE BIRDS WITH ONE STONE.

I WOULD'VE BEEN CAUGHT IF YOU HADN'T WARNED ME.
ALL RIGHT.
WE'LL FOLLOW THEIR MOVEMENTS FROM HERE. KEEP YOUR DISTANCE AND STAND BY.
DOPPLE.
GOT IT.
"FLY ON THE WALL": SILENT WORKER!
BLIP BLIP
THEY'RE STAYING IN MASADORA.
NOW WE CONFIRM CARDS.
96
CLAIRVOYANT SNAKE
A-12
FEED IT A CARD RANK C OR ABOVE, AND IT WILL SPIT UP A "CLAIRVOYANCE."

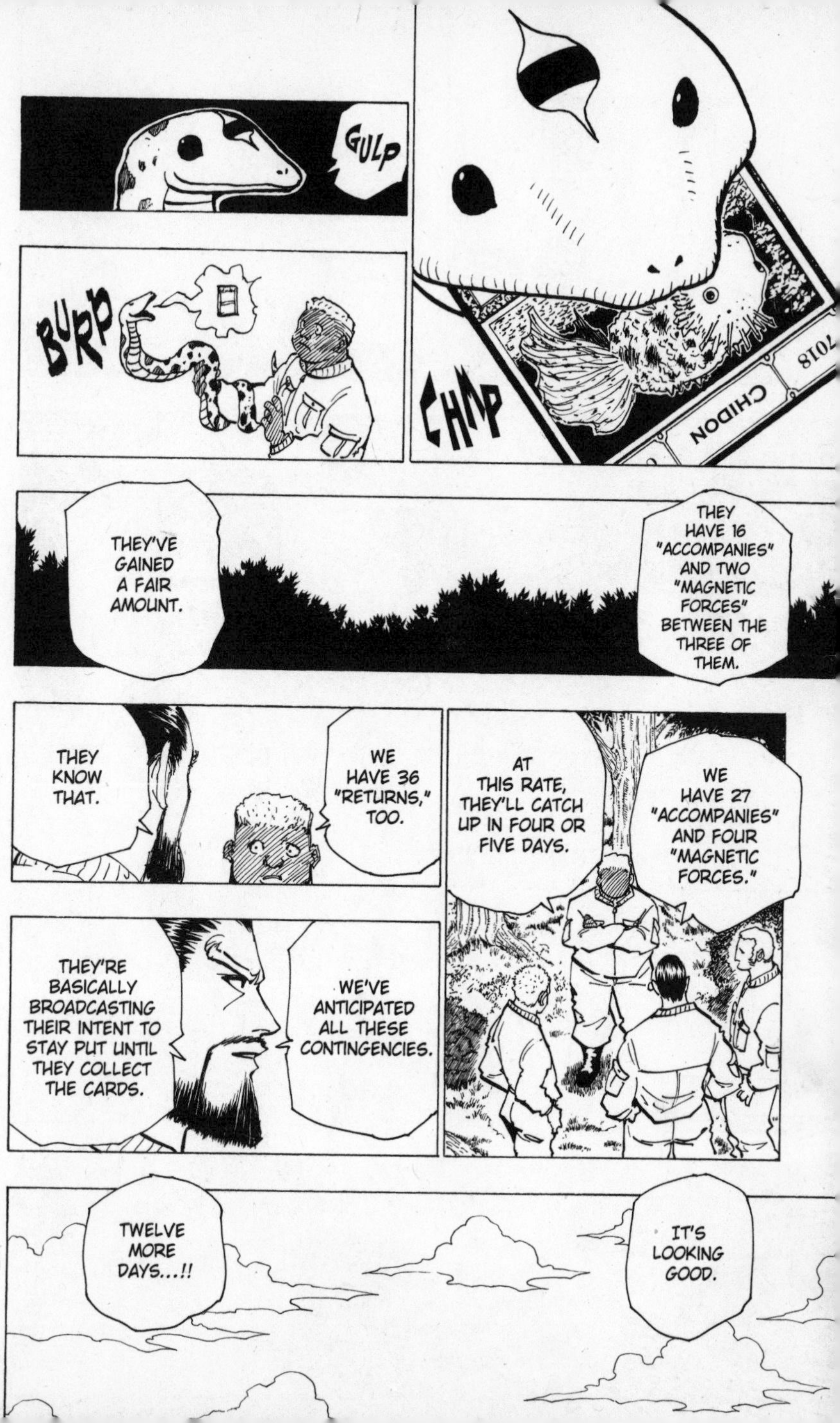
CHMP
CHIDON
7018
GULP
BURP
THEY HAVE 16 "ACCOMPANIES" AND TWO "MAGNETIC FORCES" BETWEEN THE THREE OF THEM.
THEY'VE GAINED A FAIR AMOUNT.
WE HAVE 27 "ACCOMPANIES" AND FOUR "MAGNETIC FORCES."
AT THIS RATE, THEY'LL CATCH UP IN FOUR OR FIVE DAYS.
WE HAVE 36 "RETURNS," TOO.
THEY KNOW THAT.
WE'VE ANTICIPATED ALL THESE CONTINGENCIES.
THEY'RE BASICALLY BROADCASTING THEIR INTENT TO STAY PUT UNTIL THEY COLLECT THE CARDS.
IT'S LOOKING GOOD.
TWELVE MORE DAYS...!!

PLIP
HAH !!!
...
WOBBLE
POUF...
I CAN'T DO IT...
WHUD

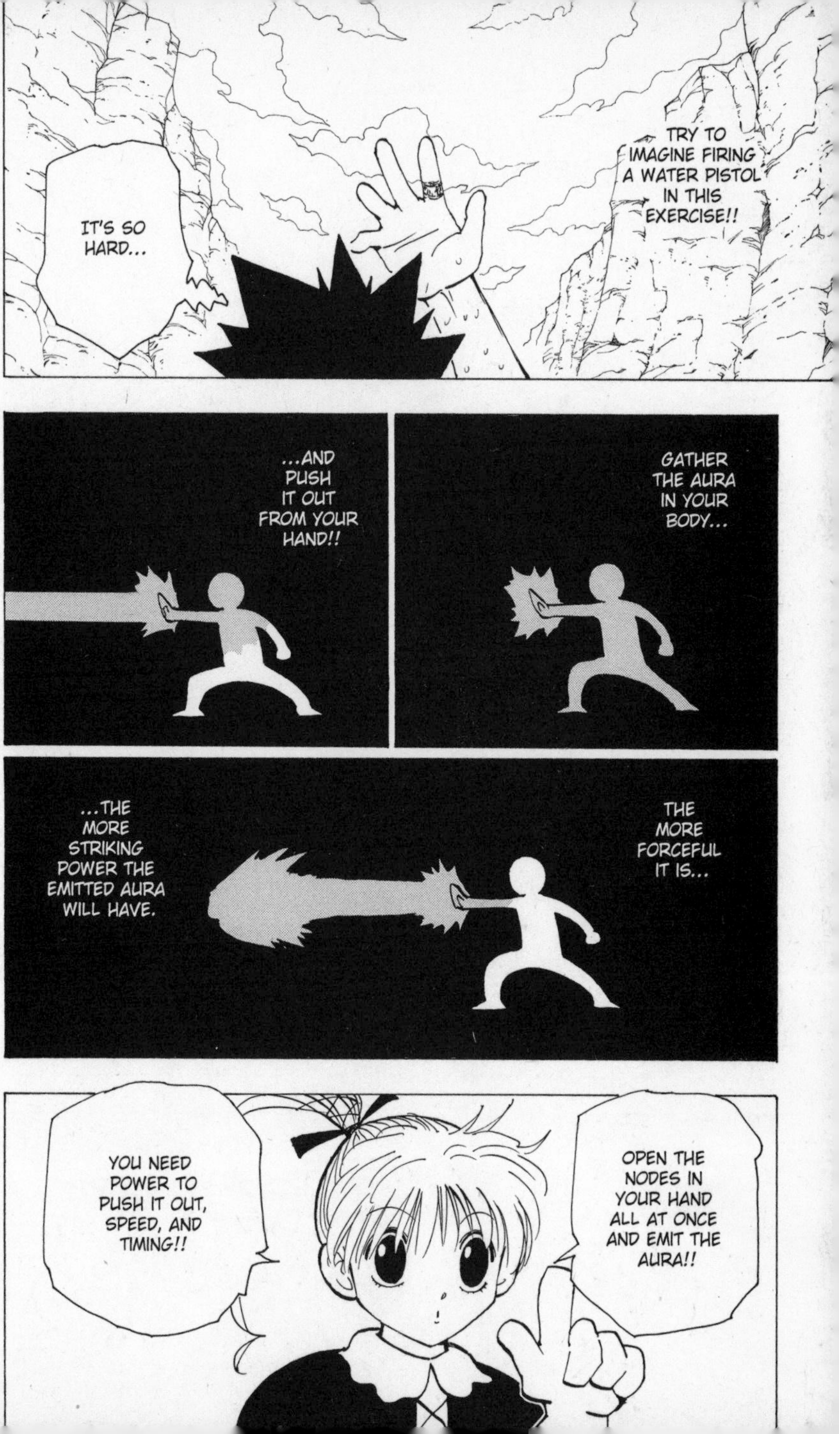
TRY TO IMAGINE FIRING A WATER PISTOL IN THIS EXERCISE!!
IT'S SO HARD...
GATHER THE AURA IN YOUR BODY...
...AND PUSH IT OUT FROM YOUR HAND!!
THE MORE FORCEFUL IT IS...
...THE MORE STRIKING POWER THE EMITTED AURA WILL HAVE.
OPEN THE NODES IN YOUR HAND ALL AT ONCE AND EMIT THE AURA!!
YOU NEED POWER TO PUSH IT OUT, SPEED, AND TIMING!!

OR ELSE YOU WON'T GET THE EFFECT YOU WANT.
IT'S REALLY HARD TO *PUSH* THE AURA FROM MY HAND.
HE'S HAVING A HARD TIME.
HE'S NEVER CONTROLLED THE FLOW OF AURA IN HIS BODY BEFORE.
THERE HASN'T BEEN ANY PROGRESS IN TEN DAYS.
MAYBE HE SHOULD'VE GONE STEP BY STEP.
WE STILL HAVE TEN MORE DAYS.
THAT DEPENDS ON TSEZGUERRA.
MAYBE THAT TRADE WASN'T SO WISE.
THEY'LL ONLY BE TWO CARDS AWAY ONCE WE GIVE THEM NO. 75.
BESIDES NO. 0.
TRY HARDER!
WE STILL HAVE 30 CARDS TO GO.

JUST TAKE THEM FROM GENTHRU.
BY FORCE.
GON WON'T AGREE TO THAT.
ANYWAY, WE GOTTA FORMALIZE OUR PLAN.
THAT'S TRUE.
IS THIS BIG ENOUGH?
YEAH.

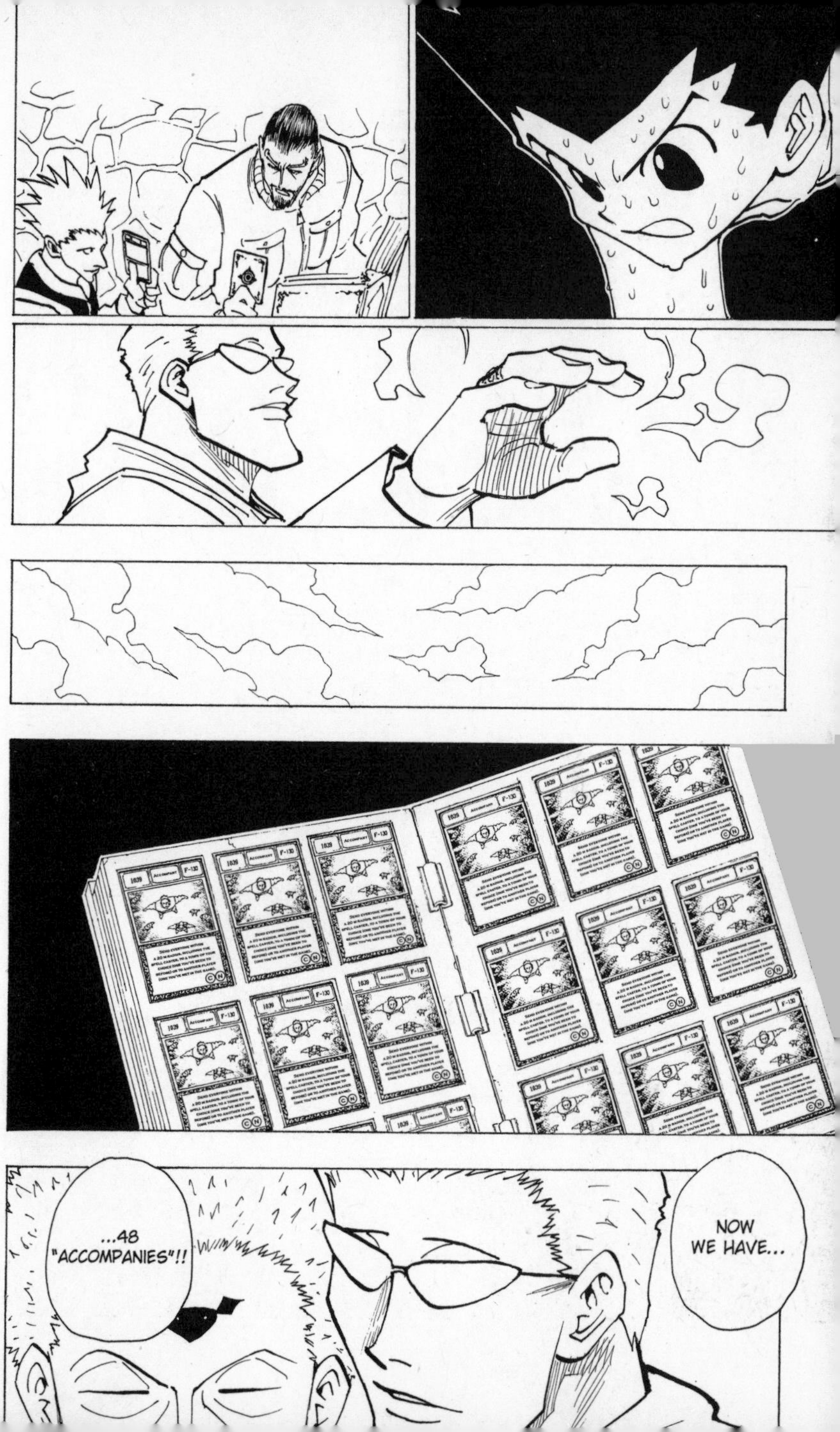
NOW WE HAVE...
...48 "ACCOMPANIES"!!

THEY ONLY HAVE 45 EQUIVALENTS OF "ACCOMPANY," "RETURN," AND "MAGNETIC FORCE."
THEY CAN'T SHAKE US.
THIS IS A GAME OF TAG...
ONE WHERE WE KNOW HOW IT'LL END.
"ACCOMPANY" ON!!
TSEZGUERRA!
!!
THEY'RE ON THE MOVE!!
COMING FAST!!
THEY'RE HERE.
SHEEN

Chapter 170
Three-Way Struggle: Part 4

"ACCOMPANY" ON!!
TO MASADORA!!
Z-OOM!!
"ACCOMPANY" ON!!
TSEZGUERRA!!
SHOO

READ THIS WAY
SHOOOM
I'M OUT!! BARRY!
GOT IT!!
1039
ACCOMPANY
F-130
SEND EVERYONE WITHIN A 20 M RADIUS, INCLUDING THE SPELL CASTER, TO A TOWN OF YOUR CHOICE (ONE YOU'VE BEEN TO BEFORE) OR TO ANOTHER PLAYER
MET IN THE GAME).
"ACCOMPANY" ON!!
TO SOUFRABI!!

HOW MANY LEFT?
SEVEN "ACCOMPANIES."
THEY STOPPED CHASING. DID THEY GIVE UP...?
NO.
THEY'RE CHANGING THE PACE TO KEEP US GUESSING.
USE "RETURN" ONCE "ACCOMPANY" IS OUT.
I KNOW. ALTERNATE BETWEEN AIAI AND SOUFRABI.
"CONTACT" ON! GOREINU!!
THIS IS TSEZGUERRA. HOW GOES IT?
IT WAS EXACTLY LIKE YOU SAID.
SUB AND BARA JUST SHOWED UP.
THEY'RE LOOKING FOR ME AT THE SPELL CARD SHOP AGAIN.

GENTHRU'S CHASING YOU WITH TWO *IMPOSTORS* RIGHT NOW.
THEY FIGURED I'D GO SHOPPING WHILE THEY'RE BUSY PLAYING TAG.
THEY MUST'VE SWITCHED OUT SOMEWHERE ALONG THE WAY.
YOU WERE RIGHT.
WE WON'T FALL FOR THE SAME TRICK TWICE.
ISN'T IT OUR CHANCE TO STRIKE? GENTHRU WILL HAVE NO HELP.
AGAINST US *FOUR!*
NO...
WE SHOULD MAXIMIZE OUR CHANCES.
WE'LL STICK TO OUR PLAN...!
SHEEE
TWOO WUV!
TWOO WUV!
HERE THEY COME!
THE GAME IS BACK ON.

SHEEEEEEE
HAH!!!
...
POUF...
ARGH!
WE ONLY HAVE FIVE DAYS LEFT...
IT'S NOT WORKING.
CAN'T YOU GIVE HIM SOME KIND OF ADVICE?
THE SENSATION OF AURA FLOWING INSIDE YOUR BODY FEELS DIFFERENT FOR EVERYONE.
I DON'T WANT TO GIVE HIM PRECONCEPTIONS AND CONFUSE HIM FURTHER. IT MIGHT BACKFIRE.

GON.
TIME'S UP.
STOP PRACTICING.
WHAT?
WE STILL HAVE FIVE DAYS!
CHANGE OF PLANS.
UM, I'M REALLY CLOSE...
MAYBE...
YEAH RIGHT. YOU CAN'T FOOL US.
WE CAN'T USE SOMETHING WE CAN'T COUNT ON.
GIVE UP.
...
WE'VE FORMED A STRATEGY TO BEAT THEM.
AND THERE'S SOMETHING WE NEED YOU TO DO.
BUT!
BUT...

WE'LL USE THIS.
YOU'LL PRACTICE 24/7...
...UNTIL YOU CAN GET IT PERFECTLY.
HERE'S THE PLAN...
SHEEEN

ZNK!!
THAT WAS OUR LAST "ACCOMPANY"!
USE "RETURN"!!
FSHH
"RETURN" ON! TO AIAI!!
1009 RETURN
ZOOOM!!
THEY'RE OUT OF "ACCOMPANY."
IT'S ENDGAME.

SHOOOM
ANOTHER PLAYER HAS CAST "CONTACT" ON YOU.
DID YOU GET ANY?
JUST ONE.
AND A TOTAL NEWBIE TO THE GAME.
EVERYONE'S HEARD THE BOMBER'S HUNTING PLAYERS HERE. NOBODY'S SHOWING UP.
TSEZGUERRA'S SUPPLIER MUST'VE BEEN AMONG THE GUYS WE'VE KILLED ALREADY.
MAYBE...
OKAY, COME BACK. I'M IN SOUFRABI RIGHT NOW.
THEY'RE OUT OF CARDS...
...AND OUT OF LUCK.

1014
LEAVE
B-30
SEND ONE PLAYER OFF THE ISLAND.
OUR LAST OPTION.
"LEAVE"...!!
IF THEY COME AFTER US, WE'LL GET THEM IN THE CASTLE.
IF NOT, WE'LL JUST WAIT UNTIL THE PROMISED DAY.
PERFECT.
TIME TO PICK THE THREE CARDS WE GET AS PRIZES...!
WE SHOULD ASK MR. BATTERA WHICH ONES HE WANTS.
SHEEE
LET'S GO.
"LEAVE"!!
1014
LEAVE
B-30
SEND ONE PLAYER OFF THE ISLAND.

FsHH...
NOBODY'S HERE...?!
WHAT'S GOING ON?! WHERE ARE THE ARMED GUARDS?!

SABAZUSHI!! WHERE ARE YOU?!
ANSWER ME!!
GIMME A BREAK. I JUST WENT TO BED.
!!
BED?! WHERE'S EVERYONE ELSE?!
THEY LEFT.
...
WHA...?
BATTERA CANCELLED THE CONTRACT HIMSELF.
I ALREADY GOT MY CANCELLATION FEE, BUT I STUCK AROUND TO LET YOU KNOW.
WHAT THE...?

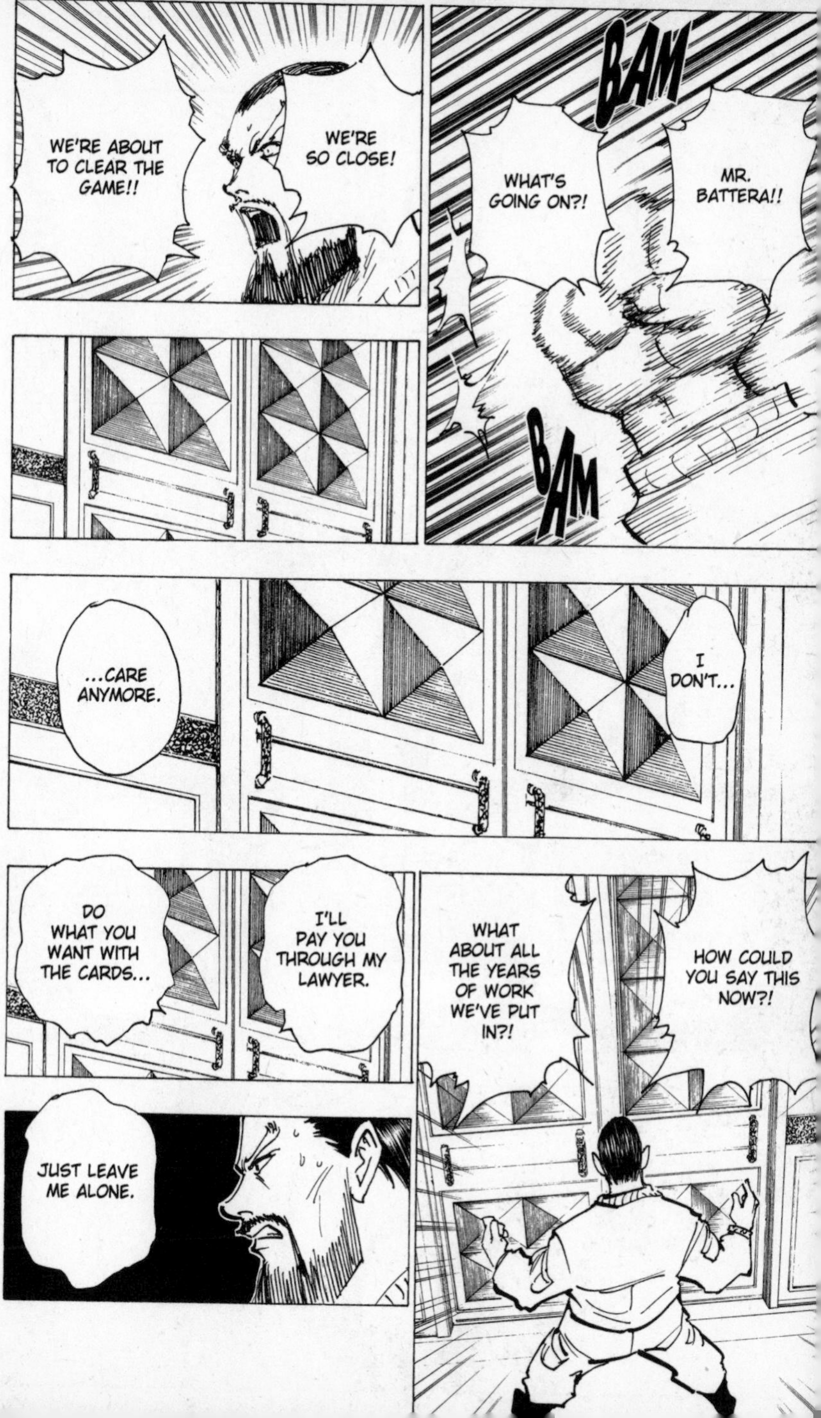
BAM
MR. BATTERA!!
WHAT'S GOING ON?!
BAM
WE'RE SO CLOSE!
WE'RE ABOUT TO CLEAR THE GAME!!
I DON'T...
...CARE ANYMORE.
HOW COULD YOU SAY THIS NOW?!
WHAT ABOUT ALL THE YEARS OF WORK WE'VE PUT IN?!
I'LL PAY YOU THROUGH MY LAWYER.
DO WHAT YOU WANT WITH THE CARDS...
JUST LEAVE ME ALONE.

READ THIS WAY

SARASA
TSEZGUERRA
BODOM
BARRY
DOPPLE
IT'S BEEN 10 DAYS...
...SINCE THEY LEFT THE GAME.
WHAT'S GOING ON?
THE THREE WEEKS WAS UP FIVE DAYS AGO.
THEY'RE GOING TO LOSE THEIR CARD DATA TODAY IF THEY DON'T GET BACK.
WE'LL HAVE TO WAIT FOR WORD FROM GOREINU.
CLIK
Chapter 170
Three-Way Struggle: Part 5

YES! PERFECT!
I GET IT RIGHT EVERY TIME NOW!!
CAN I GO BACK TO PRACTICING EMISSION?
NO!
YOU STILL HAVE AN ERROR MARGIN OF 0.1 SECONDS, DON'T YOU?
OUR IDEAL MARGIN OF ERROR IS LESS THAN THAT!! KEEP GOING!!
DRAT.
CLIK
ANOTHER PLAYER HAS CAST "CONTACT" ON YOU.
IT'S GOREINU. SORRY TO KEEP YOU WAITING.
WHAT'S UP?

YOU KNOW IT'S ALMOST BEEN 240 HOURS SINCE THEY LEFT THE GAME, RIGHT?
YEAH.
JUST SO YOU KNOW, THEY AREN'T COMING BACK.
WHY NOT?
GENTHRU IS WAITING AT THE SHISO TREE.
TSEZGUERRA HAS NO WAY TO KNOW THAT, BUT WE AGREED ON THE PLAN BEFOREHAND.
HE WON'T COME BACK UNLESS I SEND A MESSENGER TO HIS HIDEOUT...
...TO TELL HIM IT'S SAFE TO RETURN TO THE GAME.
I SEE.
BUT HE'S GOING TO LOSE HIS CARD DATA, ISN'T HE?
I HAVE ALL THE RARE CARDS.
GENTHRU MUST'VE CAST "CLAIRVOYANCE" TO CHECK THEIR CARDS! IT WOULD'VE BEEN OBVIOUS THEY WEREN'T CARRYING ANYTHING RARE. HE'LL FIND OUT ABOUT YOU!

THEY LEFT THE GAME TEN DAYS AGO AT 3:05 PM, RIGHT?
WHOOO
YEAH. WE ALL CHECKED OUR WATCHES.
THEY'LL LOSE THEIR CARD DATA IN FIVE MINUTES.
THEY'VE QUIT, FOR ALL INTENTS AND PURPOSES.
LET'S WAIT UNTIL 3:10, JUST IN CASE.
IF THEY'RE NOT BACK BY THEN, THEY'VE GIVEN UP.
...
DO YOU REALLY THINK THEY'D QUIT?
WE KNOW THOSE FOUR HAVE BEEN WORKING TOGETHER THE PAST 20 YEARS.
THAT HASN'T CHANGED SINCE THEY ARRIVED ON GREED ISLAND.
THEY GAVE UP BECAUSE THEIR PLAN TO AMBUSH US FAILED.
THEY TOOK OFF WITH BATTERA AS A LAST DITCH EFFORT TO KEEP US FROM GETTING THE REWARD.

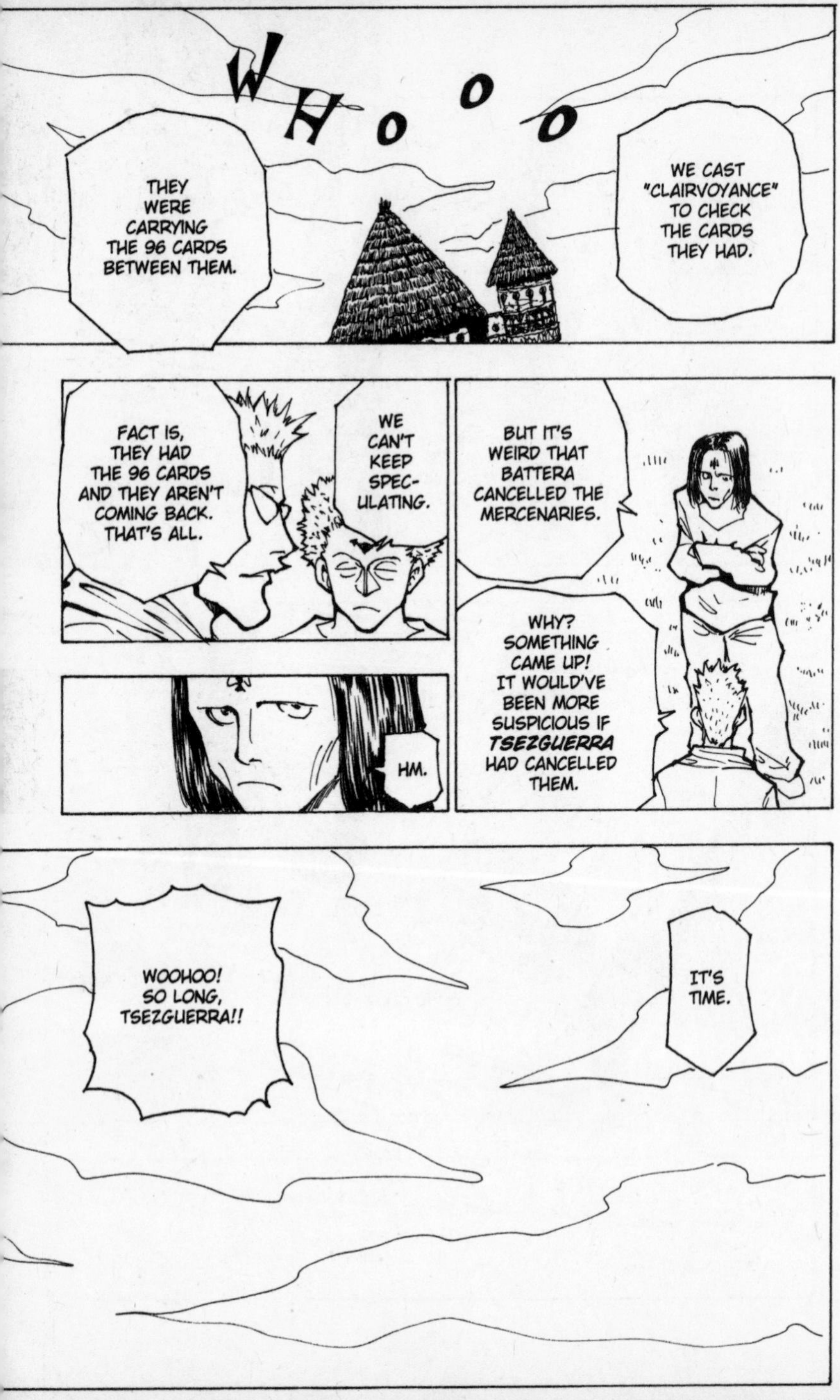

WHOOO
WE CAST "CLAIRVOYANCE" TO CHECK THE CARDS THEY HAD.
THEY WERE CARRYING THE 96 CARDS BETWEEN THEM.
BUT IT'S WEIRD THAT BATTERA CANCELLED THE MERCENARIES.
WHY? SOMETHING CAME UP! IT WOULD'VE BEEN MORE SUSPICIOUS IF *TSEZGUERRA* HAD CANCELLED THEM.
WE CAN'T KEEP SPEC-ULATING.
FACT IS, THEY HAD THE 96 CARDS AND THEY AREN'T COMING BACK. THAT'S ALL.
HM.
IT'S TIME.
WOOHOO! SO LONG, TSEZGUERRA!!

TIME TO GET THE KIDS.
WE'LL HAVE TO GET THE "PLOT OF BEACH" FROM THEM, TOO.
WE SHOULD GO TO MASADORA FIRST.
RIGHT, TO PROCURE MORE "ACCOMPANIES."
1039
ACCOMPANY
F-130
SEND EVERYONE WITHIN A 20 M RADIUS, INCLUDING THE SPELL CASTER, TO A TOWN OF YOUR CHOICE (ONE YOU'VE BEEN TO BEFORE) OR TO ANOTHER PLAYER (ONE YOU'VE MET IN THE GAME).
C N
VOOM

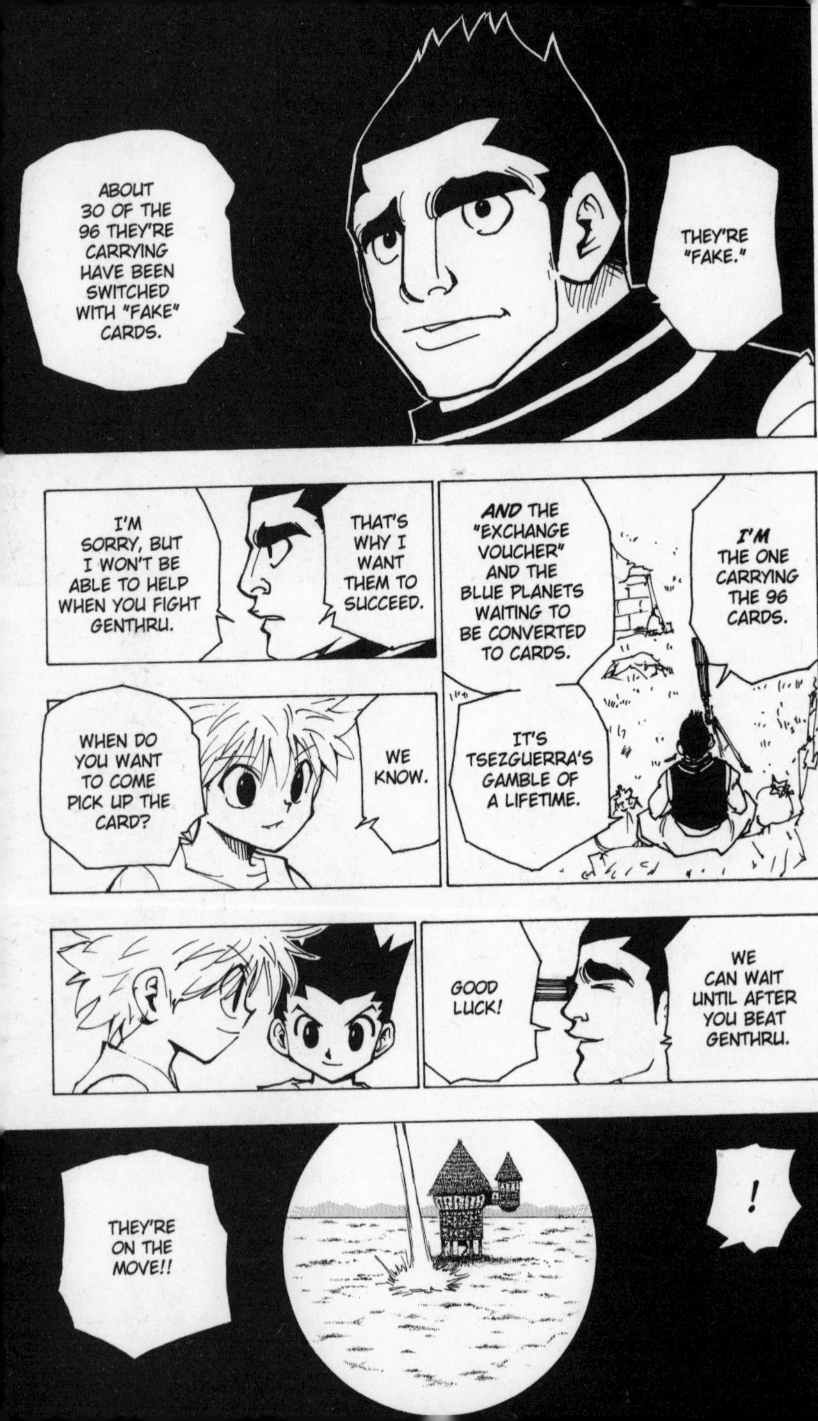
THEY'RE "FAKE."
ABOUT 30 OF THE 96 THEY'RE CARRYING HAVE BEEN SWITCHED WITH "FAKE" CARDS.
I'M THE ONE CARRYING THE 96 CARDS.
AND THE "EXCHANGE VOUCHER" AND THE BLUE PLANETS WAITING TO BE CONVERTED TO CARDS.
IT'S TSEZGUERRA'S GAMBLE OF A LIFETIME.
THAT'S WHY I WANT THEM TO SUCCEED.
I'M SORRY, BUT I WON'T BE ABLE TO HELP WHEN YOU FIGHT GENTHRU.
WE KNOW.
WHEN DO YOU WANT TO COME PICK UP THE CARD?
WE CAN WAIT UNTIL AFTER YOU BEAT GENTHRU.
GOOD LUCK!
!
THEY'RE ON THE MOVE!!

WHERE ARE YOU RIGHT NOW?!
NEAR SOUFRABI.
THEN THEY'RE GOING SOMEWHERE ELSE. MASADORA, I BET.
THEY'LL STOCK UP ON CARDS.
BUT IT WON'T BE LONG BEFORE THEY HEAD OVER.
ARE YOU READY? HOW ARE YOUR HANDS?
WE'RE ALL GOOD.
THANKS TO YOU GUYS.
IT WASN'T ENOUGH TIME TO HEAL.
BUT WE HAVE NO CHOICE.
IT'S UP TO GON NOW...
GON!
YOU DIDN'T GET DISTRACTED, DID YOU?
HOW'S THE STOPWATCH?

READ THIS WAY

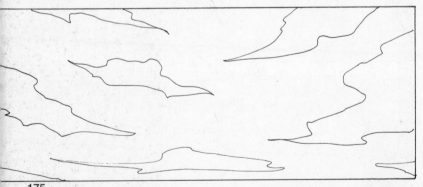

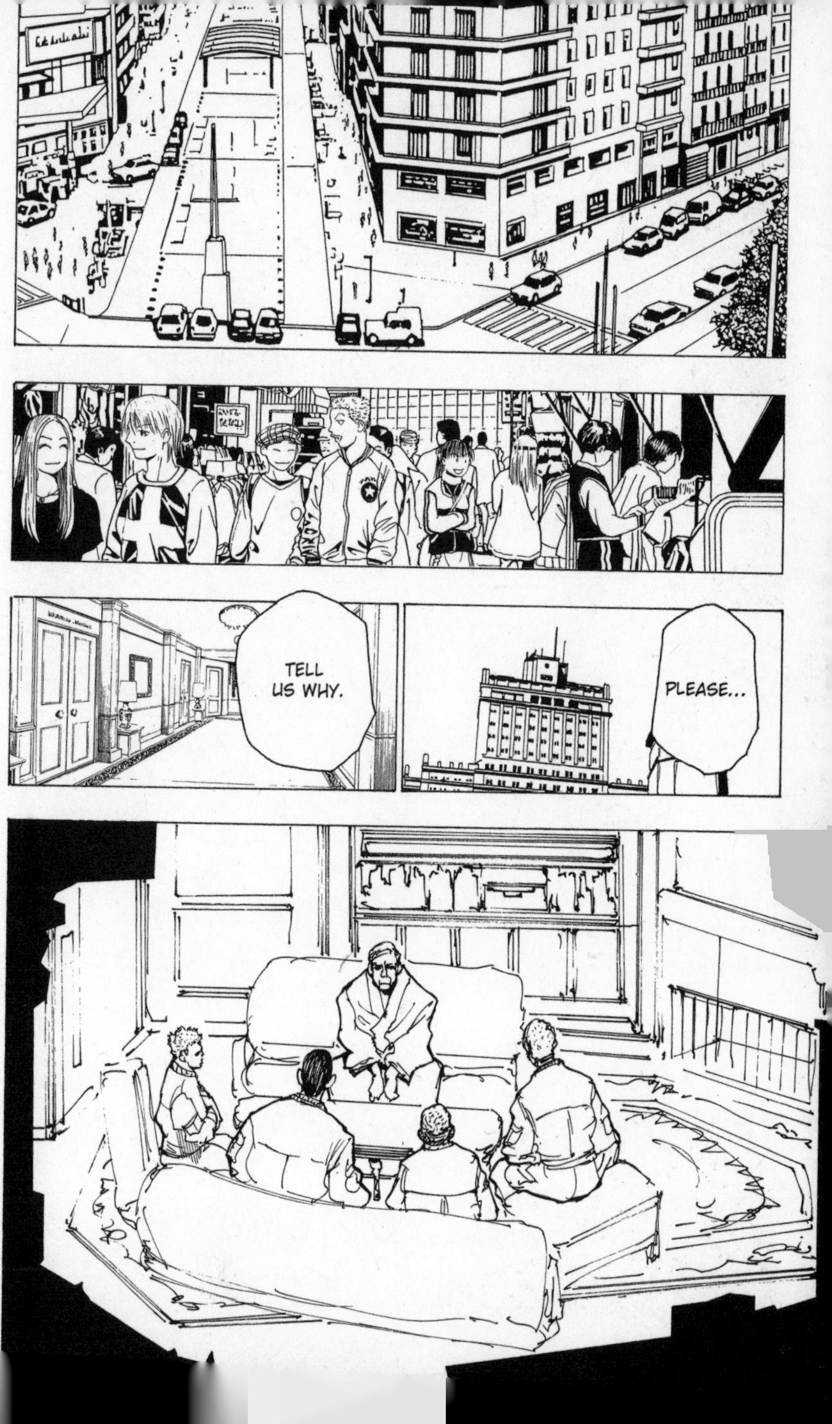
TELL US WHY.
PLEASE...

READ THIS WAY

I TOOK THE LIBERTY...
...OF TAKING THIS FROM YOUR CHAMBER.
TK...
DOES IT HAVE TO DO WITH THIS YOUNG LADY?

TELL US WHAT WENT WRONG.
PLEASE HELP US UNDERSTAND...!!
IS SHE YOUR DAUGHTER ...
...OR GRAND-DAUGHTER?
SHE WAS MY FIANCÉE.
SHE WAS IN A COMA...
...IN THE HOSPITAL FOR A LONG TIME.

READ THIS WAY

I HAD HOPE...
...THAT SHE WOULD WAKE UP AGAIN, BUT... SHE DIED LAST MONTH.
SHE DIDN'T WANT ANYONE ...
...TO THINK SHE WAS AFTER MY MONEY...
SHE REFUSED ALL THE EXPENSIVE GIFTS.
SHE PREFERRED INSTEAD THE PICTURE FRAME I CLUMSILY CARVED FOR HER MYSELF.
ALL WE NEEDED TO BE HAPPY WAS EACH OTHER.
WE HAD JUST DECIDED TO DONATE ALL MY ASSETS AND GET MARRIED, WHEN...

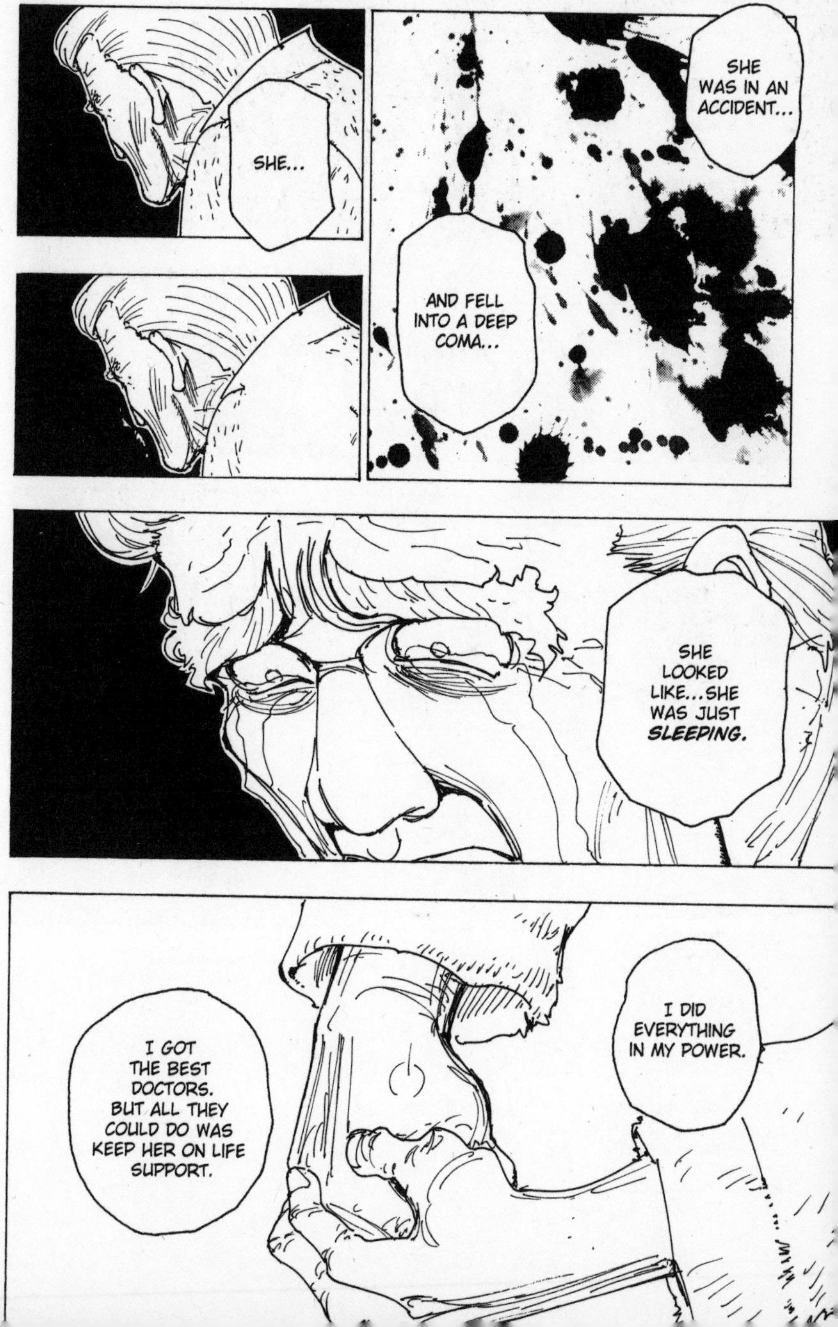
SHE WAS IN AN ACCIDENT...
AND FELL INTO A DEEP COMA...
SHE...
SHE LOOKED LIKE...SHE WAS JUST SLEEPING.
I DID EVERYTHING IN MY POWER.
I GOT THE BEST DOCTORS. BUT ALL THEY COULD DO WAS KEEP HER ON LIFE SUPPORT.

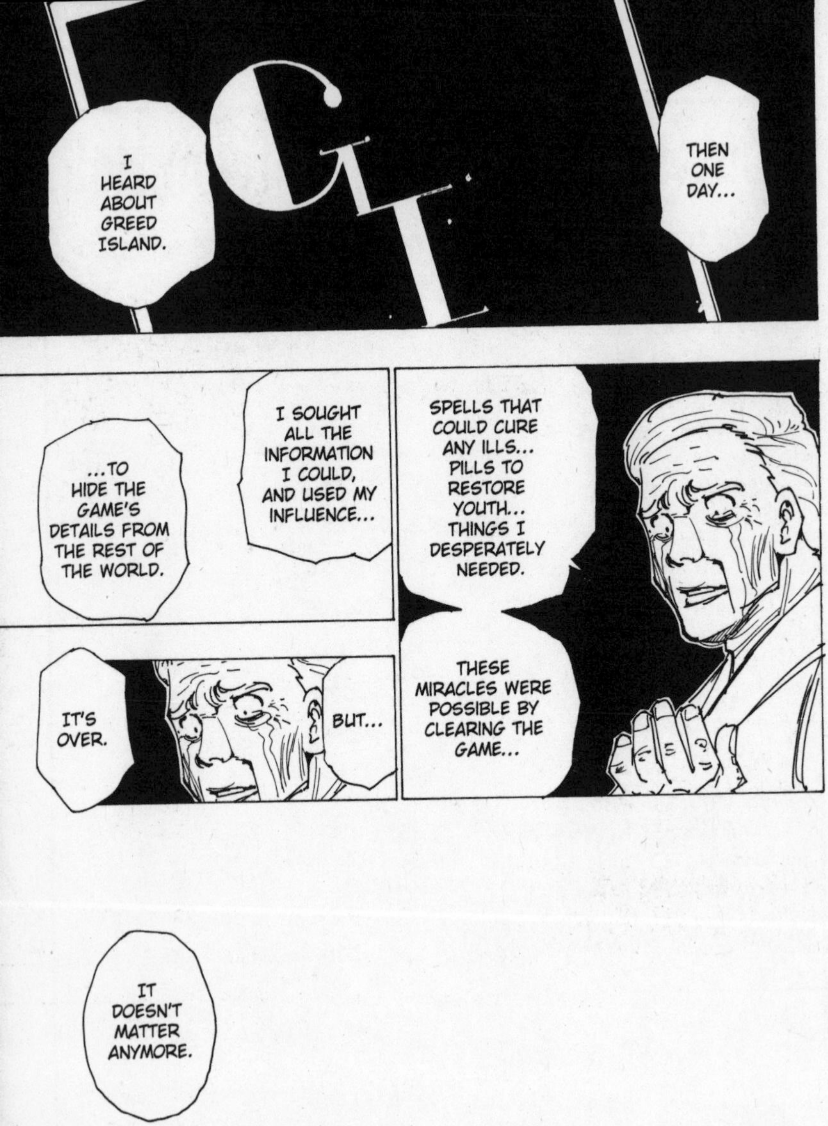
THEN ONE DAY...
I HEARD ABOUT GREED ISLAND.
SPELLS THAT COULD CURE ANY ILLS... PILLS TO RESTORE YOUTH... THINGS I DESPERATELY NEEDED.
THESE MIRACLES WERE POSSIBLE BY CLEARING THE GAME...
I SOUGHT ALL THE INFORMATION I COULD, AND USED MY INFLUENCE...
...TO HIDE THE GAME'S DETAILS FROM THE REST OF THE WORLD.
BUT...
IT'S OVER.
IT DOESN'T MATTER ANYMORE.

Hunter Exam Marathon from Hell

- TOTAL NUMBER OF PARTICIPANTS: 1266 (36 PASSED)

- DATA ON THOSE WHO PASSED:

23 MALES, 13 FEMALES

STATS:

INTELLIGENCE	HP	AGILITY	POWER	
2	3	2	3	22 PEOPLE
2	4	1	3	6 PEOPLE
2	3	3	2	1 PEOPLE
2	3	1	4	3 PEOPLE
3	3	2	2	4 PEOPLE

FIVE PEOPLE PASSED WITH HP INTACT.

YOUNGEST: 10 YEARS OLD (THREE OF THEM)

OLDEST: 41 YEARS OLD

PLEASE COMPARE WITH P.198-199!

- THE NUMBER OF PEOPLE WHO FAILED AT EACH POINT:

①	153
②	51
③	11
④	28
⑤	16
⑥	67
⑦	3
⑧	24
⑨	440
⑩	24
⑪	22
⑫	38
⑬	4
⑭	37
⑮	56
⑯	16
⑰	24
⑱	81
⑲	12
⑳	105
㉑	9
㉒	9

Chapter 170
Three-Way Struggle: Part 6

THEY HAVE THREE "ACCOMPANIES" BETWEEN THEM.
PLUS ONE "RETURN" EACH. SO FOUR EQUIVALENTS.
WE HAVE SIX. SHALL WE GO?
WE'RE READY ANY TIME.
I'LL TAKE THE KID WITH THE BLACK HAIR.
THAT'S IF IT COMES DOWN TO FORCE, OF COURSE.
SUB, YOU TAKE THE WHITE-HAIRED ONE.
BARA, TAKE THE GIRL.
"ACCOMPANY" ON!!
1039
ACCOMPANY
F-130
SEND EVERYONE WITHIN A 20 M RADIUS, INCLUDING THE SPELL CASTER, TO A TOWN OF YOUR CHOICE (ONE YOU'VE BEEN TO BEFORE) OR TO ANOTHER PLAYER (ONE YOU'VE MET IN THE GAME).
C N
GON!!

SHEEEN
ZNK!!
FSHHH...
Chapter 170
Three-Way Struggle: Part 6

WHAT DO YOU WANT?
DON'T BE SO HOSTILE.
WE'RE HERE TO NEGOTIATE.
YEAH RIGHT...!
WE WON'T TALK TO YOU!
WE CAN'T LET THEM KNOW...
...THAT WE'VE BEEN WAITING, FULLY PREPARED...!

DON'T BE LIKE THAT. IT'S NOT A BAD DEAL.
IT'S SUCH A GOOD IDEA, EVEN TSEZGUERRA AGREED TO IT.
WHAT IS IT?
WANT TO HEAR ME OUT?
WE'D LIKE TO GET CLOSER.
NO!!
YOU CAN TALK FROM THERE!
GOOD...
WE HAVE TO SEEM WEAK AND IGNORANT.
YOU LIAR.
WE MUST GIVE THEM THE IMPRESSION...
...THAT WE ARRIVED *THERE* AFTER BEING CORNERED IN A CHASE...!
IT'S SIMPLE.
WE SPLIT THE REWARD.

THE THREE OF US CLEAR THE GAME...
...ON EVERYONE'S BEHALF, GO BACK TO BATTERA, AND SPLIT THE LOOT EVENLY.
EASY, RIGHT?
I CAN'T TRUST YOU.
AFTER ALL THOSE THREATS YOU MADE?
WE TURNED OVER A NEW LEAF.
IN FACT, TSEZGUERRA'S BACK IN THE REAL WORLD NOW. LOOK IT UP.
WE KNOW THAT.
BUT THAT'S NOT PROOF THAT YOU STRUCK A DEAL WITH HIM.
GUESS THAT'S TRUE.
THEN WHAT?
YOU WANNA DIE RIGHT HERE?
BRR
WHY DON'T YOU SHUT UP AND HAND OVER THE CARDS?
OR WE'LL KILL YOU.

HE'S SHOWN HIS TRUE COLORS!!
"ACCOMPANY" ON!!
1039
ACCOMPANY
F-130
SEND EVERYONE WITHIN A 20M RADIUS, INCLUDING THE SPELL CASTER, TO A TOWN OF YOUR CHOICE (ONE YOU'VE BEEN TO BEFORE) OR TO ANOTHER PLAYER (ONE YOU'VE MET IN THE GAME).
C N
TO SOUFRABI!!
BOOM!!
HEH HEH, THEY HAVE TWO LEFT.
THEY HAVE NO "MAGNETIC FORCES" OR "LEAVES." WHAT WILL THEY DO?
ONE MORE...
THEY'RE OUT...!
"RETURN" ON! TO MASADORA!!

ZOOM!!
MASADORA... TO GET MORE SPELL CARDS?
NO... THEY'LL GO WEST!
THEY'RE GOING TO LEAVE THROUGH THE HARBOR.
"ACCOMPANY" ON! GON!!
SHOOOM
BLOOP
BLOOP
ZINK!!

WHERE'D THEY GO?
BLOOOP
BLOOOP
THEY CAN'T BE FAR.
IN THE BUSHES?
THEY HID.
I HADN'T THOUGHT OF THIS ONE.
CHECK THE SHOP!
WE DON'T WANT THEM TO GET CARDS.
NOT HERE.
SEE, THEY MUST'VE GONE WEST.
THEY COULD STILL BE HIDING.
ALL RIGHT, WE'LL HAVE TO CHECK.

HFF
HFF
SHF
SHF
HEH HEH, WELL? IS IT OVER ALREADY?
JUST GIVE UP AND GIVE US YOUR CARDS.
...

NO WAY.
WE'D NEVER GIVE THEM TO YOU!
LIKE WE THOUGHT...
THEY WANT TO FIGHT ONE-ON-ONE.
I'D RATHER FIGHT...
...THAN HAND THEM OVER!!
GON!!
THIS IS CRAZY ...!
NOW, LEAD THEM AWAY FROM EACH OTHER...!
SHF

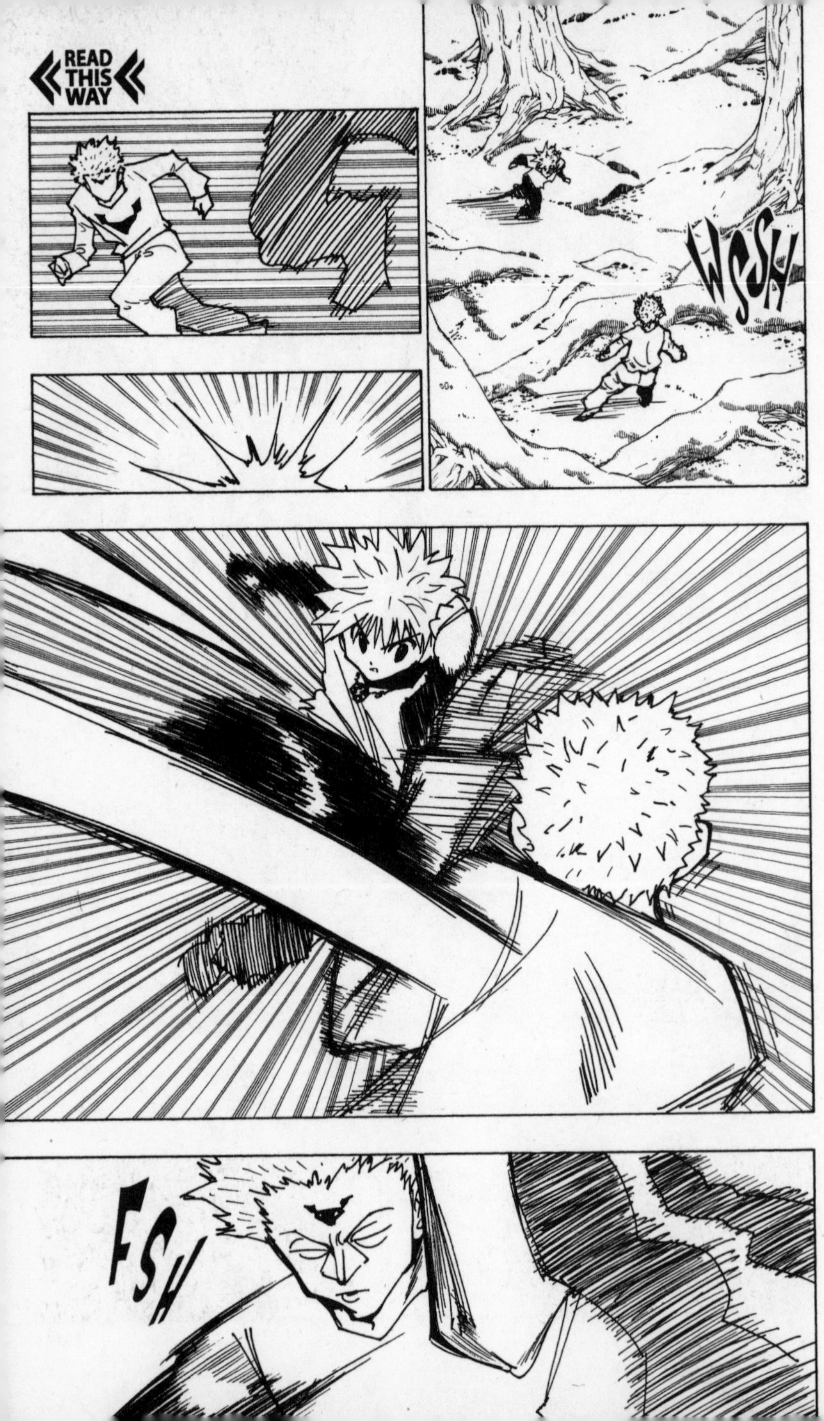
READ THIS WAY
WSSH
FSH

BAM
STING
I CAN'T USE MY HANDS...
...BUT THEY WON'T HINDER ME EITHER!
BISCUIT, RUN!!
BUT...
BUT--
SAVE YOURSELF!!

Vol. 17: Three-Way Struggle: END.

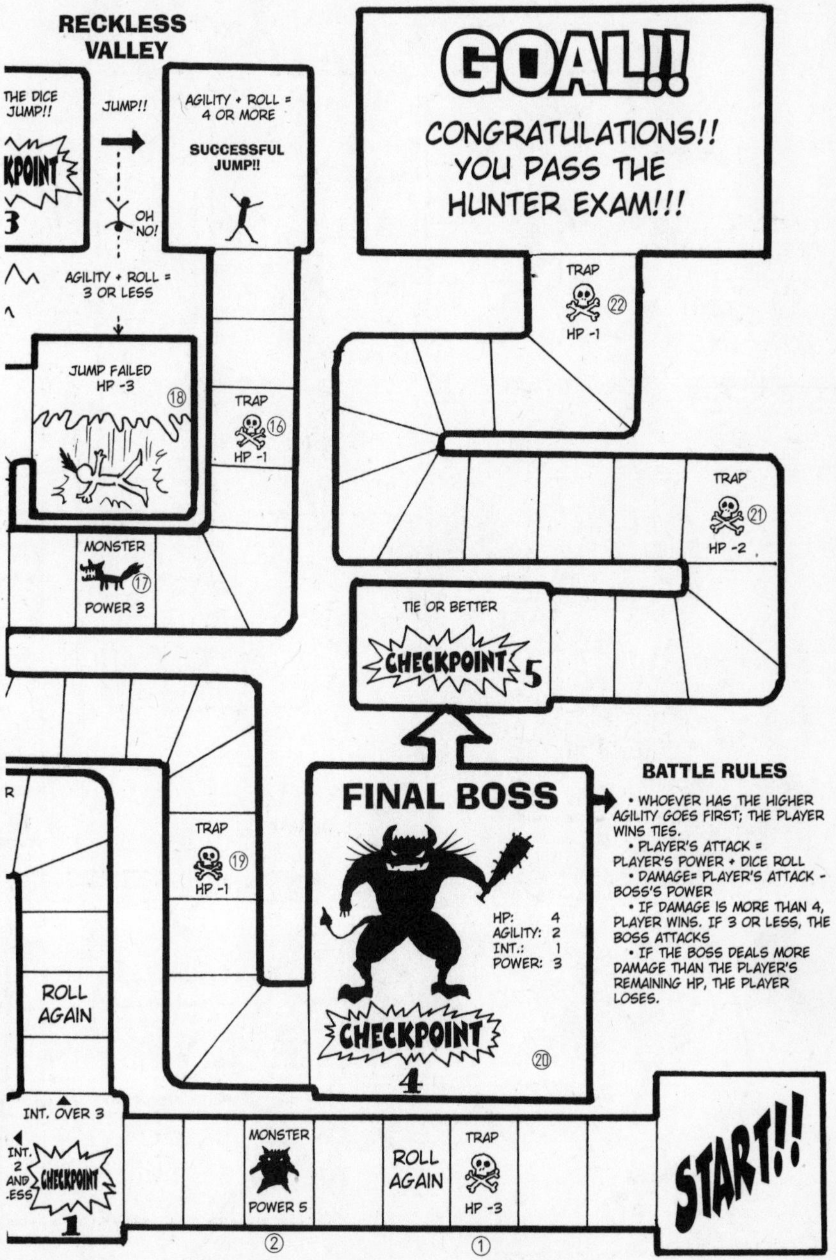
RECKLESS VALLEY
THE DICE JUMP!!
KPOINT
3
JUMP!!
OH NO!
AGILITY + ROLL = 3 OR LESS
AGILITY + ROLL = 4 OR MORE
SUCCESSFUL JUMP!!
JUMP FAILED HP -3
⑱
TRAP
⑯
HP -1
MONSTER
⑰
POWER 3
GOAL!!
CONGRATULATIONS!! YOU PASS THE HUNTER EXAM!!!
TRAP
㉒
HP -1
TRAP
㉑
HP -2
TIE OR BETTER
CHECKPOINT 5
FINAL BOSS
HP: 4
AGILITY: 2
INT.: 1
POWER: 3
CHECKPOINT
4
⑳
BATTLE RULES
• WHOEVER HAS THE HIGHER AGILITY GOES FIRST; THE PLAYER WINS TIES.
• PLAYER'S ATTACK = PLAYER'S POWER + DICE ROLL
• DAMAGE= PLAYER'S ATTACK - BOSS'S POWER
• IF DAMAGE IS MORE THAN 4, PLAYER WINS. IF 3 OR LESS, THE BOSS ATTACKS
• IF THE BOSS DEALS MORE DAMAGE THAN THE PLAYER'S REMAINING HP, THE PLAYER LOSES.
TRAP
⑲
HP -1
ROLL AGAIN
INT. OVER 3
INT. 2 AND LESS
CHECKPOINT
1
MONSTER
POWER 5
②
ROLL AGAIN
TRAP
HP -3
①
START!!

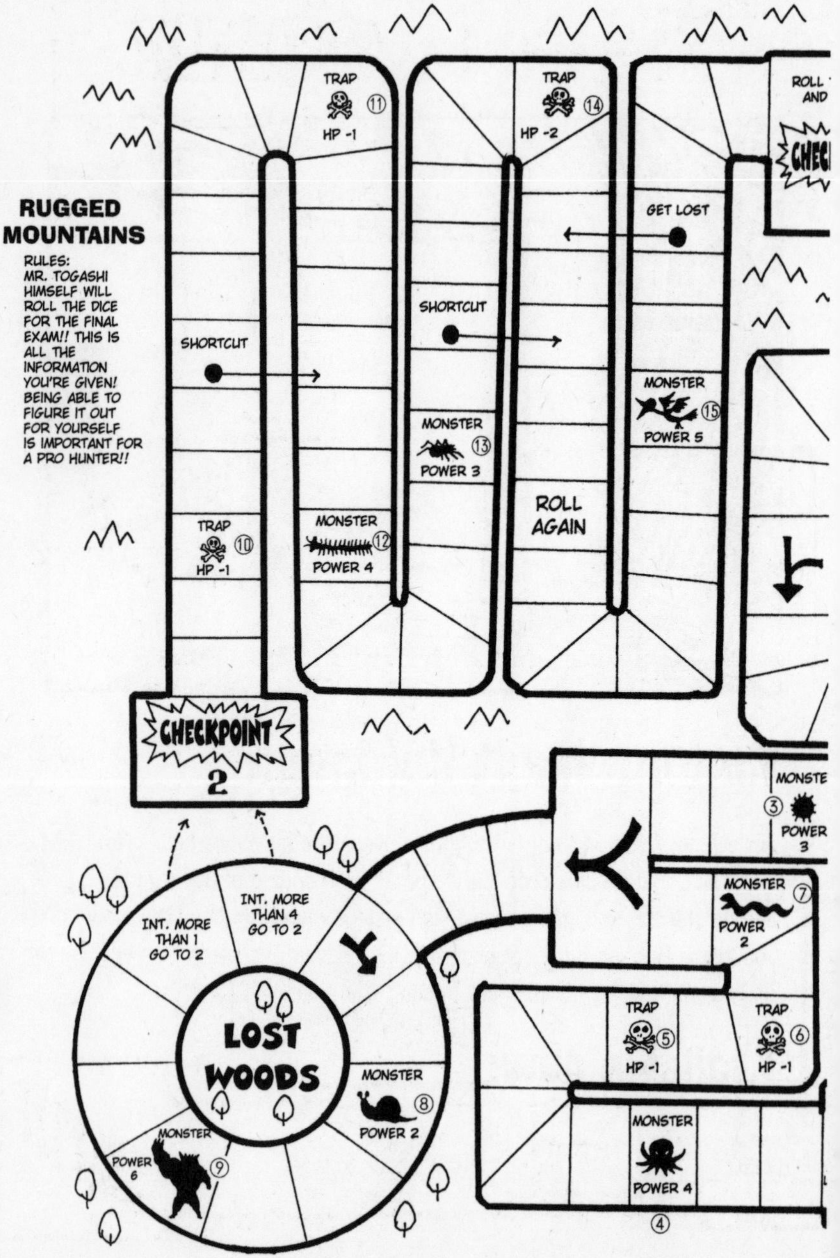

RUGGED MOUNTAINS
RULES:
MR. TOGASHI HIMSELF WILL ROLL THE DICE FOR THE FINAL EXAM!! THIS IS ALL THE INFORMATION YOU'RE GIVEN! BEING ABLE TO FIGURE IT OUT FOR YOURSELF IS IMPORTANT FOR A PRO HUNTER!!
TRAP ⑪ HP -1
TRAP ⑭ HP -2
ROLL
AND
GET LOST
SHORTCUT
SHORTCUT
MONSTER ⑮ POWER 5
MONSTER ⑬ POWER 3
ROLL AGAIN
TRAP ⑩ HP -1
MONSTER ⑫ POWER 4
CHECKPOINT 2
③ POWER 3
MONSTER ⑦ POWER 2
INT. MORE THAN 4 GO TO 2
INT. MORE THAN 1 GO TO 2
LOST WOODS
TRAP ⑤ HP -1
TRAP ⑥ HP -1
MONSTER ⑧ POWER 2
MONSTER POWER 6 ⑨
MONSTER POWER 4
④

Coming Next Volume...

Hello face, meet Mr. Fist! The fight against the bombers gets crazy, and Killua and Biscuit drop the hammer on a couple of adversaries. During the dust-up, Biscuit reveals her true shocking form! It'll blow you away! But the fun's not over yet, as a revenge-seeking Gon will stop at nothing to get payback against the heartless Genthru!

Available now!

SJ
Change Your Perspective–Get BIG
Rurouni Kenshin
Nobuhiro Watsuki
SHONEN JUMP MANGA
1
Three in One
Rurouni Kenshin
Nobuhiro Watsuki
Relive Kenshin's journey with the new VIZBIG Editions, featuring:
•Three volumes in one
•Exclusive cover designs
•Color manga pages
•Larger trim size
•Color artwork
•Bonus content
And more!
See why Bigger is Better—
start your VIZBIG collection today!
SHONEN JUMP
www.shonenjump.com
VIZBIG EDITION
Available at your local bookstore and comic store
RUROUNI KENSHIN © 1994 by Nobuhiro Watsuki/SHUEISHA Inc.
RATED T+ FOR OLDER TEEN
ratings.viz.com
VIZ media
www.viz.com

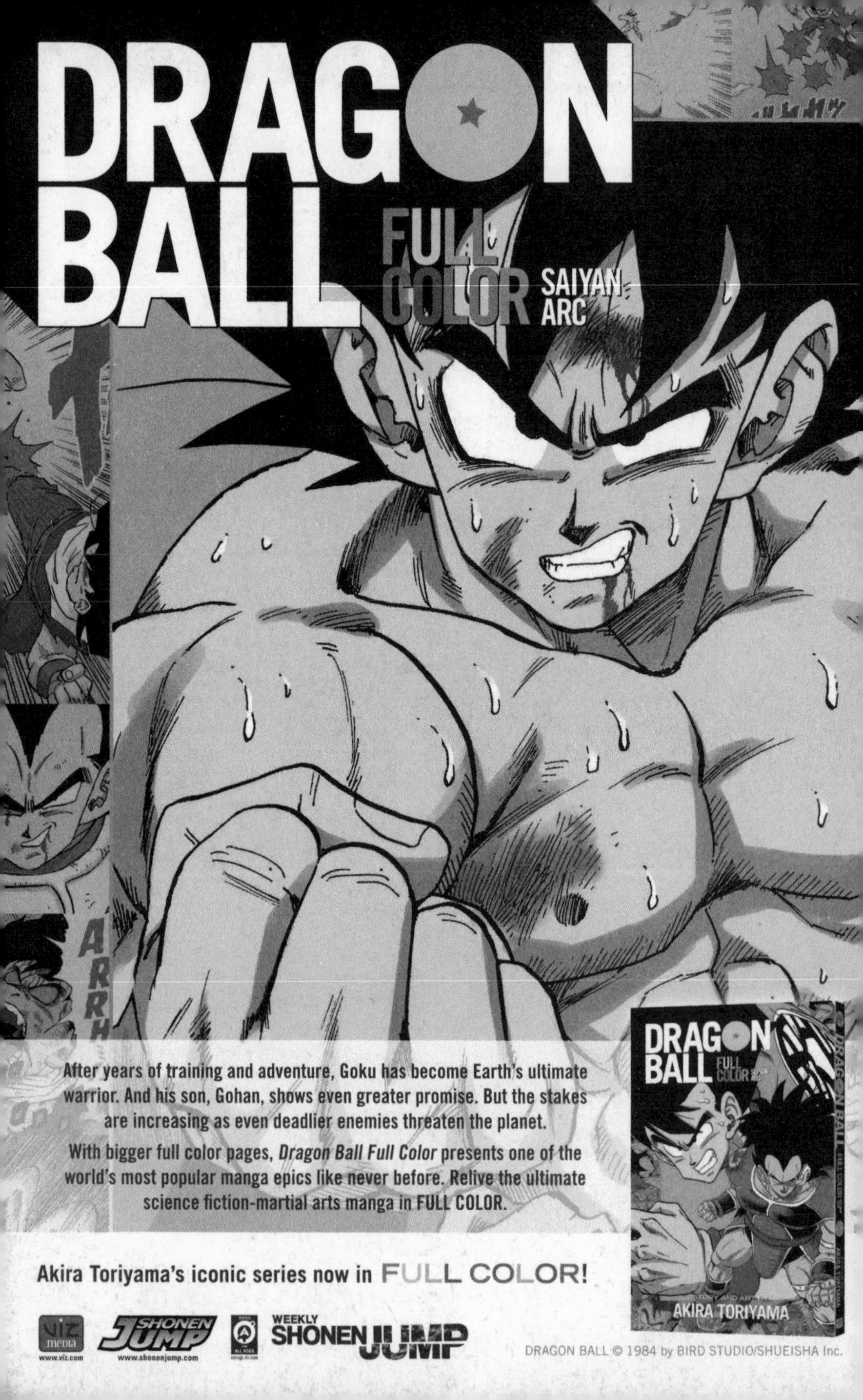

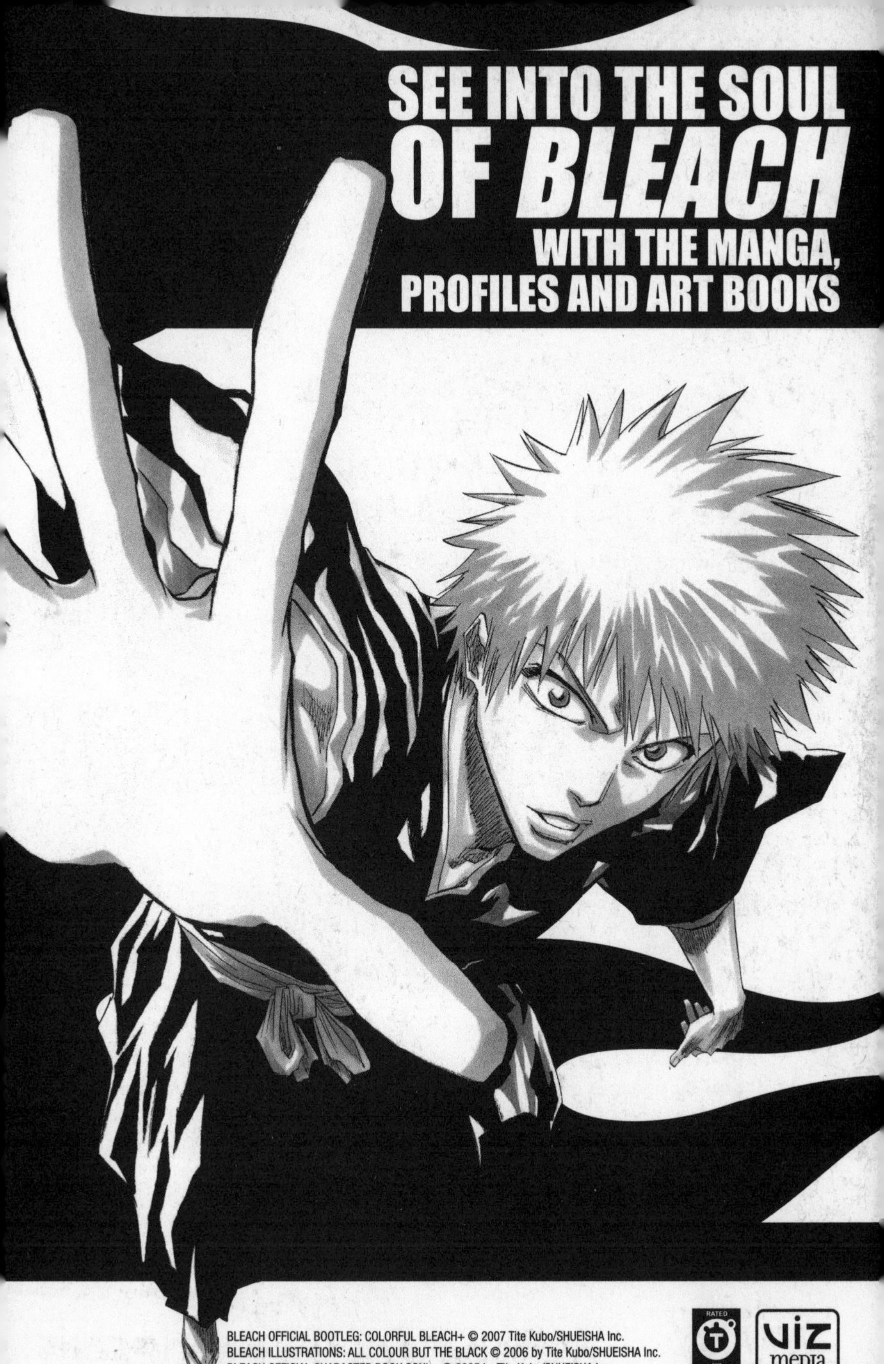
SEE INTO THE SOUL
OF BLEACH
WITH THE MANGA,
PROFILES AND ART BOOKS

You're Reading in the Wrong Direction!!

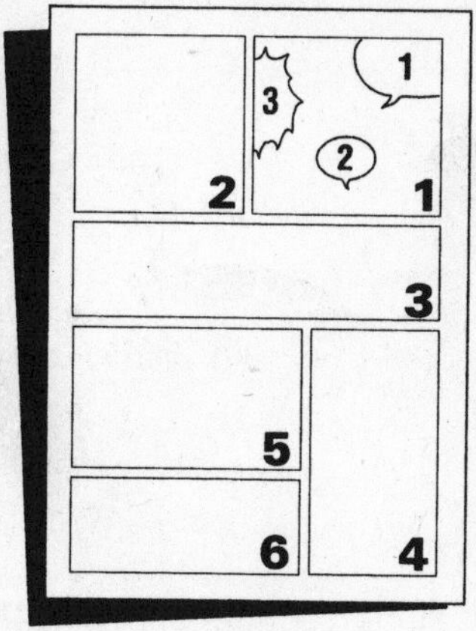

Whoops! Guess what? You're starting at the wrong end of the comic!

...It's true! In keeping with the original Japanese format, **Hunter x Hunter** is meant to be read from right to left, starting in the upper-right corner.

Unlike English, which is read from left to right, Japanese is read from right to left, meaning that action, sound effects and word-balloon order are completely reversed... something which can make readers unfamiliar with Japanese feel pretty backwards themselves. For this reason, manga or Japanese comics published in the U.S. in English have sometimes been published "flopped"—that is, printed in exact reverse order, as though seen from the other side of a mirror.

By flopping pages, U.S. publishers can avoid confusing readers, but the compromise is not without its downside. For one thing, a character in a flopped manga series who once wore in the original Japanese version a T-shirt emblazoned with "M A Y" (as in "the merry month of") now wears one which reads "Y A M"! Additionally, many manga creators in Japan are themselves unhappy with the process, as some feel the mirror-imaging of their art skews their original intentions.

We are proud to bring you Yoshihiro Togashi's **Hunter x Hunter** in the original unflopped format. For now, though, turn to the other side of the book and let the adventure begin...!

—Editor